BIRMINGHAM AT PLAY

Alton & Jo Douglas

The Scala Cinema, Smallbrook Street, 11th October 1955.

ISBN 1 85858 040 4
Published by Brewin Books, Doric House, Church Street, Studley, Warwickshire B80 7LG.
Printed by Warwick Printing Co. Ltd., Theatre Street, Warwick CV34 4DR.
Layout by Alton & Jo Douglas.

Queensbridge Operatic Society, from Kings Heath, get in shape at the Corinthian Gymnasium, Smallbrook Ringway, for their production of "Orpheus in the Underworld", shortly to open at the Old Rep, Station Street. 1st May 1981. The gym is now called Curves & Co.

Front cover: A second Silver Jubilee street party for the residents of Dainton Grove, Bartley Green, 2nd June 1978. The previous year's celebrations had been so successful that the neighbours decided to do it all over again a year later!

CONTENTS

TOWN HALL BIRMINGHAM
Telephone: Central 2392

6.30 SATURDAY, 23rd JANUARY, 1965 8.0

RONALD SMITH presents FOR ONE NIGHT ONLY

TOP BEAT '65

with BIRMINGHAM'S OWN SENSATIONAL

ROCKIN' BERRIES

THEIR LATEST PYE HIT — 'WHAT IN THE WORLD'S COME OVER YOU ?'

BRITAIN'S TOP FEMALE SINGER

JULIE ROGERS

and THE HI-FI's

LATEST HIT – "LIKE A CHILD"

PRETTY THINGS "DON'T BRING ME DOWN"

THE SORROWS "I DON'T WANNA BE FREE" (PICCADILLY)

CARL WAYNE AND THE VIKINGS Pye Recording Artists | **TOM JONES AND THE SQUIRES**

Compere: TONY MARSH

TICKETS: 12/6 10/6 7/6 5/- AVAILABLE FROM THE BOX OFFICE AND USUAL AGENCIES

Patron
Her Majesty The Queen

we the undersigned
tender our sincere congratulations to

Bryan "Chuck" Botfield

on being one of the representative artistes
selected to appear before

Her Majesty Queen Elizabeth

on the occasion of the

Royal Variety Performance

held at the

London Palladium

on Monday, November 13th, 1967

the performance being in aid of the
Variety Artistes' Benevolent Fund

The Rockin' Berries – from Town Hall dates to Royal Variety shows – stars of the sixties, seventies, eighties and now, with this current line-up, the nineties.

YOUNGER THAN SPRINGTIME

Elsie and Winnie Grice, Cato Street North, Saltley, 1903

Children from the Cottage Homes, Erdington, arrive at Rhyl for their annual outing, c. 1925.

It's amazing how much fun centred around a lamp-post! The swing on the left looks quite an elaborate set-up. Trent Street, Bordesley, 1910.

Parents' Day Concert, Conway Road Junior School, Sparkbrook, 1931.

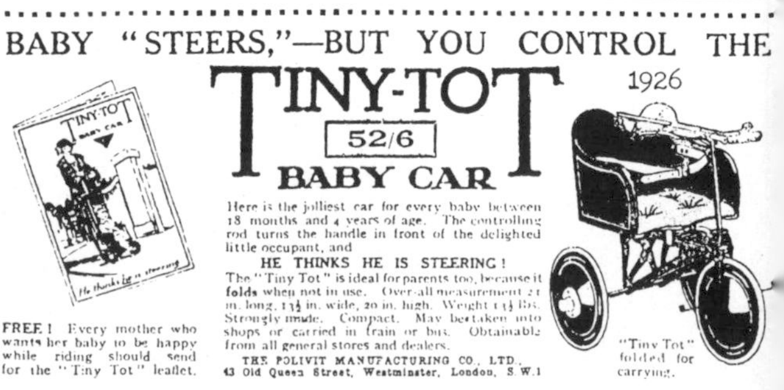

A trip to The Lickeys, by children from Broad Street Presbyterian Church, c. 1932.

Modern Gym Form Pageant, King Edward's VI Grammar School for Girls, Handsworth, 1933.

St Andrew's scouts and cubs, Bordesley, 1936.

Senior football team, Bournville Elementary School, 1934/5.

Loxton Street School, Bloomsbury, 1935.

Birmingham Schools' Netball Rally, Botanical Gardens, Edgbaston, 1942.

Winners of the Aston and North Birmingham Sports' Shield, Rookery Road Junior School, Handsworth, 1946.

Sir,—I support Mr. Charles H. Bond in his appeal to the City Parks Committee to allow the Scouts' Rally to be held in Handsworth Park again this year; but there should be a condition in the contracts (this also applies to the Birmingham Show) that contractors must clear up the inevitable mess.

The damage caused to the precious turf by heavy lorries and hundreds of tent and tubular poles driven into the ground is distressing to Handsworth residents and nature-lovers generally. The holes should be filled up and the turf replaced before contractors leave the ground.

H. BROWNING BUTTON.
47, Lansdowne Road,
Handsworth, Birmingham 21.

[The Parks Committee has now given permission for the Rally to be held in Handsworth Park this year—though not in succeeding years.—Editor.] 1945

Christmas Party, Joseph Lucas Ltd., Great King Street, Hockley, 1947.

After the concert, the four girl dancers and their audience pose for the camera, YWCA, Dame Elizabeth House, Richmond Road/Bordesley Green East, Stechford, 1944.

Swimming team, Rookery Road Junior School, Handsworth, 1949.

Skiffle group, Carpenters Road, Lozells, Summer 1953.

Hypnotised by a Punch and Judy Show, Selly Park Recreation Ground, 1953.

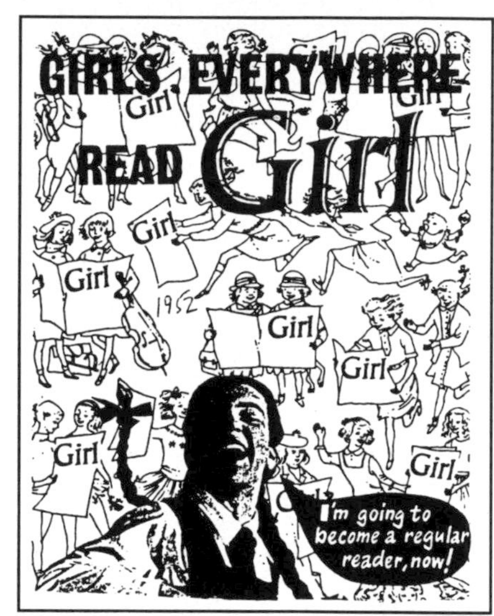

Just some of the children holidaying under the Christopher Robin scheme at Butlin's Camp, Pwllheli, c. 1954. Rob Pryke and Lilian Home had the idea of taking parties of Kings Norton children to the seaside each year.

FORMED HIS OWN BOYS' BRIGADE COMPANY

Two years ago, there was no such thing as the 12th Birmingham Company of the Boys' Brigade, to-day, this company is a flourishing branch of the youth organisation with a band that is one of its most active sections.

Credit for this achievement must go to 34-year-old Traffic employee, Mr. Arthur Garbett—or Captain Garbett as the boys of the 12th Company know him, founder and present leader of the company.

Mr. Garbett has been an officer in the Boys' Brigade for 7 years and was Lieutenant in the 55th Birmingham Company before he formed his own group. His interest in the movement has grown with the years, for even as a boy he served in the ranks.

Six months after it had been founded, the company formed its own band which proved a great success. Mr. Garbett has a sound knowledge of music and was fully competent to teach the boys the use of the various instruments.

Two nights each week, Mr. Garbett is occupied teaching the boys first aid, signalling, physical training, and general training, and on Sunday mornings he conducts the bible class, together with another senior officer.

The boys have been to camp two years in succession, but Mr. Garbett is proud of the fact that through their own efforts this year they were able to go to camp on their own, instead of having to share with another company.

Mr. Garbett is married and has two sons, aged six and twelve years, and the older boy will be joining the company later this year. AUG 1954

12th Birmingham Company Boys' Brigade Band, on parade in Blake Lane, Bordesley Green, August 1954.

Let them sing!

MOBILE broadcasting units have been busy recently visiting schools in all parts of the country to take recordings with which to build up a programme for sound radio called "Let the children sing." It will form part of the Christmas week offerings by the Light. There will be a different choir each evening, and on December 23 choirs from the Midlands take over. Two come from Birmingham — those of Solihull and Selly Oak

For the task of introducing this programme of traditional songs and carols, the Light has chosen Bob Arnold—actor (he plays Tom Forrest, the gamekeeper, in "The Archers") and singer who, since his youth, has collected Cotswold folk song. 1955

Girls' Life Brigade cadets, with Moseley Arts School in the background, c. 1954.

Anthony Road Primary School cricket team, Saltley, 1956.

Cannon Hill Park, c. 1956.

Sunday school outing for the children of Ladywood to Habberley Valley, Kidderminster, 1958.

Life Boys parade along Kings Road, Kingstanding, c. 1958.

May Day celebrations, Raddlebarn Junior and Infants' School, Gristhorpe Road, Selly Oak, 1958.

Betty Fox, one of the city's most famous dance teachers, runs through a pantomime number with the Betty Fox Babes, 23rd October 1959.

6th Birmingham Company Boys' Brigade, Poplar Road, Kings Heath, 1958.

If this corner is missing this programme will admit one child only.

1686 BOURNVILLE VILLAGE

CHILDREN'S FESTIVAL

Men's Recreation Ground, Linden Rd. Bournville
(by kind permission of Messrs. Cadbury Bros. Ltd.)

Arranged and produced by the
BOURNVILLE VILLAGE COUNCIL
SATURDAY, 27th JUNE, 1964
Mr. and Mrs. C. B. TAYLOR will be present

The Festival Queen, Wendy Shakespeare, after her crowning, surrounded by local children, Children's Festival, Bournville, 27th June 1964.

"Peter Pan", Perry Beeches Junior School,
Great Barr, c. 1966.

Small Heath Park, Coventry Road,
1st June 1967.

Christmas Party, Midland Red Club, Quinton, 1968.

ALREADY well-established as the author of more than a dozen children's books, Barbara Sleigh started to write an account of her childhood in Birmingham.

She came in for a good deal of friendly warning. "No one," said one literary acquaintance, "will publish a book for adults that ends when the heroine is 15 years old."

In fact, Miss Sleigh's autobiography of her Edgbaston growing-up, The Smell of Privet (Hutchinson, £2) was published, amid some critical interest, this week.

Born in Acocks Green "when it was still a little country village," she grew up in Birmingham when it was also growing. 1970

St Vincent's Roman Catholic School, Vauxhall Grove, Nechells, 1971.

Friday afternoons represent a musical interlude for the young musicians of Grove Vale School, Monksfield Avenue, Great Barr, 5th February 1971.

THE deposit on the family-sized bottle of "pop" supplied by a leading manufacturer in the Birmingham area will be sixpence from Monday.

Today an official of the mineral water industry predicted that all other manufacturers would be following suit.

First to put up the charge from the present 3d. is Masons of Smethwick.

The company has been forced to increase the deposit because of the present-day cost of the bottles, and the fact that fewer are being returned.

OCT 1971

The relief of playtime! St Thomas' Junior School, Granville Street, 29th January 1974.

Day Nursery, Belgravia Close, Balsall Heath, 5th February 1974.

The ford proves to be the best place on the hottest day of the year, Sarehole Mill Recreation Ground, Green Road, Hall Green, 1977.

Girls from Norma's Dancing School entertain to raise money to support play groups and other self-help organisations, Sutton Coldfield, 2nd March 1979.

Because of the drought, the paddling pool is used as a roller skating rink, Senneleys Park, Bartley Green, 30th July 1984. Jack Struggles, the former British and world record holder for one and two miles, coaches local children.

Under-fives, from the child-minders' unit in Booth Street, enjoy themselves in a day of games, Handsworth Park, 16th June 1987.

NORTH WEST BIRMINGHAM DISTRICT
SCOUT ASSOCIATION

present the

'Handsworth' Gang Show 1983

Produced by ERNIE FITTON

Choreography by VAL ARCHER

Musical Director: PETER SMITH

at the

CRESCENT THEATRE
Cumberland Street, Birmingham

from

Monday, 14th March to
Saturday, 19th March, 1983

Nightly at 7.15 p.m. — Saturday Matinee at 2.30 p.m.

Philippa Colley, of Northfield, is saluted by her friends from the 96th Birmingham Guide Company, after receiving the Baden-Powell Trefoil (the highest award in Guiding), 29th March 1988.

Brownies, from the 187th Birmingham pack, hold presents for the elderly and needy, as part of the TV-am caring Christmas campaign, Boots, High Street, Kings Heath, 21st November 1988.

Les Cardell, (right) from Mapledene Junior School,
is the winner of a competition to name the Highland calf, Sheldon Country Park, 17th November 1989.
Along with three of his friends and Councillor Carl Rice he meets "Centenary Princess".

Once again, BRUMMAGEM BOATS proudly present

SANTA SPECIALS

Over the years, children of all ages have come to know and look forward to our Search for Santa. This year we commence our Searches on

5TH DECEMBER 1992

and trips are available each Saturday and Sunday throughout December.

OUR BOOKING OFFICE IS NOW OPEN ON 455 6163

Although we encourage all age groups, it is advisable for anyone over 16 years old to be accompanied by a child. Every child gets a present from Santa, and there are free mince pies for everyone.

Searches are £3.50 per person, babies under 3 go free, and we normally find Santa within an hour and a half.

THIS IS THE ONE & ONLY ORIGINAL "SANTA SPECIAL!" ACCEPT NO SUBSTITUTES!!

OUR BOATS ARE ALSO AVAILABLE FOR YOUR CHRISTMAS PARTY - IT'S NEVER TOO EARLY BUT IT MAY BE TOO LATE!

Brummagem Boats Ltd,
Sherborne St. Wharf
Birmingham B16 8DE

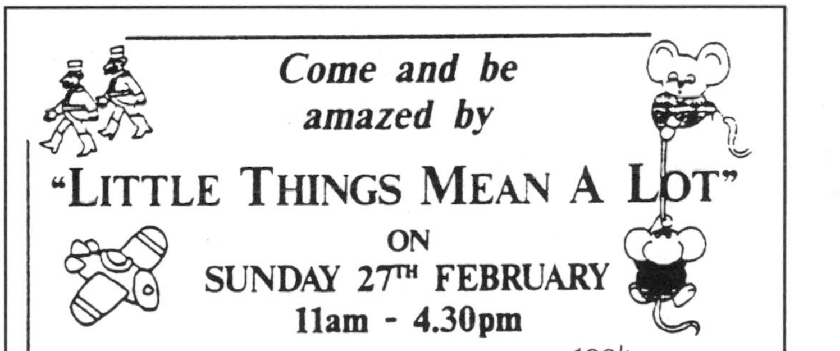

Come and be amazed by

"LITTLE THINGS MEAN A LOT"

ON
SUNDAY 27TH FEBRUARY
11am - 4.30pm
1994
AT THE
BIRMINGHAM BOTANICAL GARDENS
WESTBOURNE ROAD, EDGBASTON

INDOOR DISPLAYS
OF ALL THINGS IN MINIATURE

MODEL BOATS, CARS, PLANES & TRAINS

CLOCKS & WATCHES

DOLLS & DOLLS HOUSES

TEDDIES

MINIATURE PAINTINGS

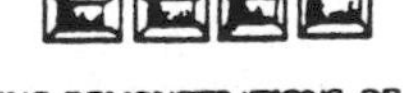

AND A DAY OF FREE ENTERTAINMENT INCLUDING DEMONSTRATIONS OF PUPPETRY, BUILDING SHIPS IN BOTTLES AND CHILDREN'S WORKSHOPS

SPECIAL GUEST: POSTMAN PAT

MINIATURE GARDEN COMPETITION

SPONSORED BY:

SPECIAL LITTLE ADMISSION PRICE
ADULTS £2.50 CONCESSIONS £1.00

MEMBERS FREE

I COULD HAVE DANCED ALL NIGHT

Fancy Dress Dance, Albert Hall, Aston, 5th February 1910.
On the original postcard it is referred to as an "Elite Social Dance" and we are reminded that this is a "flashlight photograph".

Masque Ballroom

(Proprietors Masque Dance Hall Ltd.)

WALFORD RD., SPARKBROOK
BIRMINGHAM.

Free Car Park and Dance Partners.
Private Lessons by Appointment.

Admirably suited for
Club, Staff and Works Dinners.
Charitable and Civic Functions.
Dinners and Outcomes.
Wedding Breakfasts
Whist Drives, etc.

Write for Special Terms. 1931

10 MINUTES FROM CITY CENTRE.
TRAMS—4, 17, 18, 21, 44, 89. Buses 13, 13a, 29, 30, 31.
Inner Circle Bus—No. 8.

Dance at The Masque

Studio School of Dancing

Operatic, Classical, Character & Ballroom Dancing
(Principal: HELENA LEHMISKI.)

CLASSES DAILY. YEARLY COURSES AT A SMALL INCLUSIVE FEE.
COACHING FOR ALL EXAMINATIONS—
ELEMENTARY, INTERMEDIATE, ADVANCED.
STUDENTS TRAINED FOR THE STAGE OR AS TEACHERS.
ENGAGEMENTS FOUND WHEN PROFICIENT.

For Prospectus apply:
248 Corporation Street, Birmingham.

1926

ENTERTAINING VISITORS TO THE INDUSTRIES FAIR.

The Birmingham magistrates yesterday granted an application for the extension until one o'clock on the nights of February 23 to February 26 and February 29 to March 3 of the music, singing and dancing licence in respect of the West End Dance Hall. They also gave permission for performances by a troupe provided they were limited to exhibition dances and that adequate dressing-room accommodation was provided.

An application for permission to sell intoxicants from 8 p.m. until midnight was refused.

Mr. Willison, who appeared in support of the applications, said they were made for the benefit of visitors to the British Industries Fair at Castle Bromwich. An influx of buyers was expected, and it was desirable that facilities for their entertainment should be provided.

"We should be ready to encourage this sort of thing," he said, "and realise that other towns would be only too ready to do it if they had the British Industries Fair." 1932

DANCING

FRANK DOCKER'S School of Dancing, Queen's College, Paradise-st. Mid. 2161. Private Lessons Daily 10 a.m.—9 p.m. Weekly Prac. Class to-night (Thurs.), 7.30—10.30, 2/6, at 187, Broad-st.

TONY'S BALLROOMS.

TAKE TEA AT TONY'S.

TEA DANCES DAILY, 3—6: 1/6 inc. Tea. TO-NIGHT.—RESIDENTS' NIGHT, 8—12: Adm. 2/.

ROYALE BALLROOM.—Closed to Public.

BOOK YOUR TABLES for TONY'S YULETIDE FESTIVITIES

SECRETARIES and ORGANISERS.—For Your New Year Dance TONY'S IS BEST. Book Now.

Christmas time at Tony's Ballroom, Hurst Street, c. 1932.

The Art Atkins Orchestra, Botanical Gardens, 1943.

DORIS WILLIAMS L.R.A.M.
PIANOFORTE.

Successes in all Assoc. Board R.A.M. & R.C.M. Examinations including L.R.A.M. Diplomas (Teacher & Performer). Pupils prepared for Competitions.

Dale Forty Studios &
135, Oxford Road, Moseley.
Telephone: South 2468.

ENA BARTLEY
SCHOOL OF DANCING.

Under the direction of
FREDA HARRISON, M.G.D.A., M.I.S.T.D(B.B.)
and
ELIZABETH JAMES, F.I.S.T.D(B.B.), B.B.O., (ADV) M.G.D.A., M.R.A.D.

Private lessons in Ballroom, Operatic, Greek, Tap, etc. given at any time by appointment. Training for all examinations a speciality. BALLROOM (44ft. × 34ft.) may be hired for Club Dances, Weddings or any Private Function.

Apply to the Secretary
187, BROAD STREET, BIRMINGHAM.
MIDland 4623.

E. STUART VINDEN, L.R.A.M.
(Elocution)
Receives pupils in Elocution and Dramatic Art.
MIDLAND INSTITUTE and
79, RYLAND RD., BIRMINGHAM, 15.
Telephone: CALthorpe 2868

Sonny Rose, who was the resident bandleader at the West End for many years.

The West End Cinema and Dance Hall, Suffolk Street, 16th August 1950.

AMUSEMENTS 24.2.50

CATESWELL DRILL HALL, STRATFORD ROAD, HALL GREEN. SUPERB DANCING, SATURDAY, 7.45-12.0. LES WILLIAMS AND HIS ORCHESTRA.

COME, Learn and Enjoy Real Old-Time Dancing, Powells Pool Pavilion (Boldmere ent.), Sat., 7.30-11.30, 3/6. J. Leonard Davies & Viennese Orch. KIN. 3464.

DANCING TO-NIGHT, 8.0., Stanley-Lewis School of Ballroom Dancing, 123A, Bristol Street. Private Lessons Daily. MID. 1508.

GRAND ELECTION DANCE, Sat., Feb. 25, Kingstanding Drill Hall, Kingstanding Rd., 8-12 midnight, 2/6; Lucky Spots, etc. 29, 29A, 35, 25, 34 all to door

GRESWOLDE HOTEL. DANCE EVERY SATURDAY, 8—11.30 p.m., 5/-. Dress Optional. Dinner if required. Fully Licensed until 11.30 p.m. Knowle 2488.

HARBORNE Baths Ballroom.— DANCING EVERY WED., 8 to 11, 2/-. SAT., 7.30 to 11.30, 3/-. DEN JONES AND HIS ORCHESTRA

HAWKESLEY HALL, Northfield (By Kalamazoo). DANCING, SATURDAYS, 8 to 11.30 p.m., 2/6.

HIGHFIELD, Highfield Rd., H.G. To-night, Earlswood Cycling Club Dance 8-11 o'clock. 2/6. Everybody Welcome. To-morrow: Dem. Henry Goodall & Mair Jones.

KING'S Heath Baths Ballroom. DANCING EVERY SATURDAY, 7.30 to 11.30. 2/6 CLIFF DEELEY AND HIS ORCHESTRA

MORRIS School of Ballroom Dancing, 172, Edmund St., CEN. 6397. Classes Fri., Sat., Intermed. 8-10.30. Sunday Club, members only. Mon., beginners 8-10.30.

MOSELEY & B.H. INSTITUTE. DANCING IN BALLROOM. SATURDAY, at 7.30 p..m. MONDAY, at 8 p.m. TUITION CLASS in Studio, TUESDAY at 8.0.

MOSELEY Road Baths Ballroom.— DANCING every WED., 8 to 11, 2/-. Cliff Deeley & his Orchestra. SAT., 7.30 to 11.30, 2/6. Nat Roness & his Orchestra.

NECHELLS Baths Ballroom.— DANCING EVERY WED., 8 to 11, 2/-. SAT., 7.30 to 11.30, 2/6. JIMMY DONNELLY AND HIS ORCHESTRA

NEW MEDAL CLASSES, Thursday, March 2. Bronze 7.30 p.m., Silver 9 p.m.—ALEX HOOPER SCHOOL OF DANCING, 106, Digbeth. MID. 0851.

ORANGE GROVE, Crystal Palace, Sutton Coldfield. To-morrow (Sat.): Last Heat, "Search for a Vocalist" Competition. Final Sat., March 4. Guest Star: ALAN DEAN.

SALTLEY BATHS BALLROOM. DANCING EVERY SATURDAY TO STAN WHITE AND HIS ORCHESTRA DANCING 7.30 p.m.-11.30 p.m. Admission 3/-

SMETHWICK Baths Ballroom presents 1949 Dance Band Champions of Gt. Britain every Sat. Arthur Rowberry & His Orchestra. Dancing 8-11.30. Car park. Ad. 2/6

TOWER BALLROOM. EDG. 0107.— To-night, Private Function. To-morrow, Dancing Time for Dancers. Mon. Next, George Evans & his Orches. with Judy Dean, 8 p.m. 3/-

VERNON ADCOCK PRESENTS DANCING at ST. AGNES HALL, Billesley Lane, Moseley. EVERY SATURDAY, 8 to 11. Admission 3/6.

Y. W.C.A., Dame Elizabeth House, Stechford. Dancing every Sat. Alan Melville's Band, 7.45-11, 2/6. Old-time Dancing every Tues. 7.45. Teddy Parslow's Band, 2/-.

WHIST, SATURDAY, 7.30, 2/-. Top Value £12. List Value £29. Partner Miniature, 6.45, 1/-. Top Value £5. STRATFORD ROAD SCHOOLS, SPARKBROOK

WHIST, MONDAY, 7.30. Top Value £10; 20 other Prizes. Admission 2/-. Miniature, 6.45, 6d. STRATFORD ROAD SCHOOLS, SPARKBROOK

WHIST, TUESDAY, 7.30, 2/-. SPECIAL PARTNER DRIVE. Premier Value £12. List value £31. Miniature 6.45 6d. STRATFORD ROAD SCHOOLS, SPARKBROOK

WHIST, Gower St. Schools, Lozells every Mon., £8 top, £4 2nd. Every Wed. top £10, over £20 in prizes. Adm. 2/-, 7.40. Albert Hall, Aston, every Fri., top £8. 7.40.

WHIST — WHERE TO GO EVERY SAT. & THURS., ROOKERY ROAD SCHOOLS, HANDSWORTH, 7.30 Each Night. Birmingham's Most Popular Drives.

WHIST, BIRMINGHAM'S BEST. DUDLEY ROAD SCHOOLS. EVERY SATURDAY, 7.40 p.m. PROMPT. Prize Value £30. Admission 2/-.

WHIST DRIVE, THORNTON ROAD SCHOOL, WARD END, EVERY WEDNESDAY, 7.45. Admission 2/-. Top Value £10.

WHIST, Dudley Road Schools, EVERY WEDNESDAY AND FRIDAY, 7.40 prompt. Prize value £27. Admission 2/- Buses to Door. Car Park. Refreshments.

The Atlas Assurance Company's Christmas Dance, Market Hotel, Station Street, 1953.

Staff and partners from Lloyds Bank, New Street, at an Institute of Bankers' dance, West End Ballroom, c. 1955.

The George Harris Quartet, Co-op Rooms, Alum Rock, 1959.

Fancy Dress Party, Cranbourne Road School Olde Tyme Dancing Group,
Kingstanding, New Year's Eve, 1957.

Maerika School of Dancing, Westley Road,
Acocks Green, 19th February 1962.

O YEA ! O YEA ! O YEA !

Moseley Round Table
(Society for the Preservation of
Rural Balsall Heath)

PRESENT

A COUNTRY YOKELS FROLIC

AT YE OLDE PUNCHBOWLE INNE IN
LAPWORTH COUNTY of WARWICKSHIRE
* * Stabling, Hay and Accommodation
ON THE EVENING OF

Friday July 2nd 1965

Grand Opening 8 p.m.

Hiring Fee 15/6

Dancing, Buffet, Refreshments Wet & Dry
Scrumpy, Duff and Fodder ! ! ! ! ! !

Costumes—any Rural characters—Farmers, Yokels,
Labourers, Country Gentlemen, Country Maidens !
Cowgirls, Hill Billies

COME AND JOIN THIS FEASTE OF
RUSTIC ROMP AND RURAL FROLIC ?
LATE SWIGGING ! ! ! OXCARTS 1 A.M.
Tickets not returned by June 25th will be charged

Atlas Ballroom, Flaxley Road,
Stechford, 25th November 1964

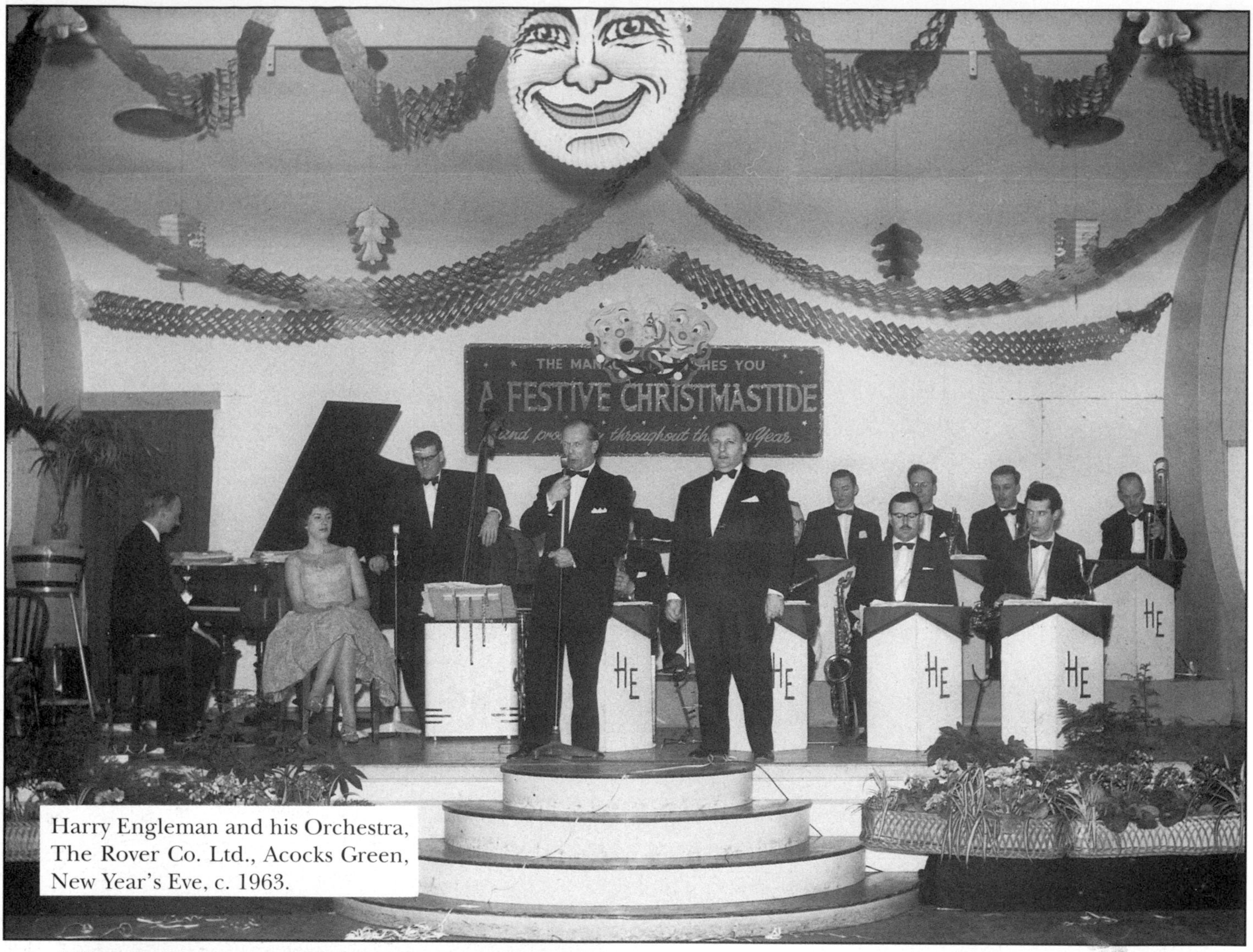

Harry Engleman and his Orchestra, The Rover Co. Ltd., Acocks Green, New Year's Eve, c. 1963.

The Alton Douglas Quartet meet members of the less-formally attired pop group, "The Hollies", Airport Hotel, Elmdon, 1966. Both groups had been hired to play for dancing at a company function.

Silver Medal Presentation, Maureen Lewis Dance Club, Bristol Street, 12th August 1967.

Birmingham musicians, The Dave Jones Nightshift, resident trio at the Supper Basket, Warwick, 1970.

The Billy Pond Ballroom and Studio, St Giles' Institute, Green Lane, Small Heath, 17th December 1974.

Ninety six year old, Philip Taylor, celebrates his birthday with his dancing partner, Val West, and members of the Galleon Dance Club, Hall Green, 1st June 1987.

THE WAY WE WERE

AN Elizabethan aircraft, Zulu Papa, has been saved from the scrapyard by Birmingham student Geoffrey Negus's love of planes.

The aircraft, which once belonged to King Hussein, of Jordan, was bought for £350 by 22-year-old Mr. Negus, of Park Road, Moseley.

Now he wants to put the aircraft on show as a museum piece near Birmingham Airport—one of the airports from which Zulu Papa flew in the 1950s.

The Decca Navigation Company used the plane for testing equipment. But earlier this year company chiefs decided the plane would have to be scrapped.

Mr. Negus, a Birmingham Polytechnic student, spotted the plane at West Malling airfield, Kent. 1973

Museum of Science and Industry, Newhall Street, 4th May 1970.

Open Day, Tyseley Railway Museum, 22nd June 1975.

Phil Mason and Keith Watkins enjoy a day at the Steam Rally, Science Museum, Newhall Street, May 1976.

Open day, Birmingham and Midland Museum of Transport, Chapel Lane, Wythall, 1984.

Prince Charles celebrates his 40th birthday, Aston Manor-Road Transport Museum, 14th November 1988.

Birmingham Museum and Art Gallery, Chamberlain Square, 1989.

Local historians gathered in Birmingham today for the first West Midlands Local History Fair.

The event, held at the city's Central Library Exhibition Hall today and tomorrow, includes displays from more than 30 groups in the Birmingham and District Association of Local History Societies, and Black Country organisations.

Historian Lord Asa Briggs launched the fair after being welcomed by the Lord Mayor of Birmingham, Coun Harold Blumenthal today.

The display will open at 11am tommorrow, closing at 5pm. 5.11.88

A model of a typical Birmingham shop made by Dave Pucci – "I created it from memories of a little shop where I once did a paper round, not far from where I lived in Heybarnes Road, Small Heath".

IT'S A GREAT DAY

Preparing for the annual Mop, Kings Norton Green, c. 1890.

BIRMINGHAM

Church of England Sunday School Association.

THE ANNUAL EXCURSION

WILL TAKE PLACE ON

Tuesday, July 5th, 1892,

TO

Stamford

And Burghley House, the Seat of the Marquis of Exeter.

Tickets: — Railway & Tea, with Meat, 5/6 each.

INCLUDING ADMISSION TO BURGHLEY HOUSE.

The Train will leave Monument Road at 7-50 a.m., calling at New Street at 8, Adderley Park at 8-4, and Leamington at 8-45 a.m.

The Return Train will leave Stamford at 7-20 p.m., and will set down at Leamington, Adderley Park, New Street, and Monument Road.

On arriving at Stamford, the Party will proceed to St. Martin's Church, where there will be a short Service and an Address to Sunday School Teachers, by the Rev. A. F. Jones, M.A.

Tea will be served in a Tent in Burghley Park, at 4-15 and 5-30 p.m.

A Cold Luncheon will be served at 12-30. in the Tent in Burghley Park, at 1/6 each, to those who drop a Post Card to Mr. J. G. Dunn, 44, Waterloo Street, Birmingham, on or before Thursday, June 30th.

A few friends gathered at a house in Birmingham a few nights ago for a convivial evening. One of them, on being called upon to sing, placed his lighted cigarette on the edge of the music-box by the side of the piano. Accidentally it got knocked off, and evidently fell among the paper in the box. Shortly afterwards the party broke up, and nothing unusual was noticed at the time; but soon afterwards the music-box and contents and half the piano were found to be on fire. The fire brigade were hastily summoned, and played the final tune upon that piano. 1908

Celebrating the end of the First World War, New Spring Street, Brookfields, 1918.

The Onion Fair, Serpentine Fairground, Aston, 1920.

MIDLAND "RED" Motor Services

1923

Take a 'Midland Red'
For Business or Pleasure

OFFICIAL TIME TABLE AND MAP—PRICE 2d.

CHEAP EXCURSIONS

TO AND FROM BIRMINGHAM AND OTHER LARGE TOWNS

ON TUESDAYS, WEDNESDAYS & FRIDAYS

TICKETS AVAILABLE ON ANY BUS

ASK CONDUCTOR FOR RETURN EXCURSION TICKET

ANYWHERE TICKETS

AVAILABLE ANY DAY EXCEPT SATURDAYS, SUNDAYS & MONDAYS

5/6 INCLUSIVE PRICE 5/6

OBTAIN TICKETS AT BULL RING OFFICE

Chief Offices: BEARWOOD Tel 3300 Mid.
Town Booking & Enquiry Office: BULL RING Tel. 386 Cent
O. C POWER Traffic Manager

City dwellers at the seaside, c. 1926.

A trip from Sparkhill to Gough's Caves, Cheddar, c. 1927.

JOSEPH CHAMBERLAIN
MEMORIAL MUSEUM

HIGHBURY, MOOR GREEN
BIRMINGHAM

OPENING CEREMONY
MONDAY, 9TH JULY, 1934

The Turner family, from Aston, visit Blackpool, 1928.
It is interesting to see that the Palace Cinema is advertising "The Talkies".

Camp Hill Gospel Hall Ladies' outing, c. 1930.

VISITED CHINESE PALACE

With my sister I went one winter to visit the ex-Emperor and Empress of China. We went with a friend of ours who was teaching the Emperor to speak English. We were able to converse with them as we could speak Chinese then—we have forgotten most of it now. For tea we had very sweet, hard, sugary cakes and sweets. Afterwards we went on to the verandah and fed the monkeys. Before we left we were each given a beautiful square of silk which we still have, together with some photographs which were taken when we were there.—Jumbo McCullagh, 362, Moseley-road, Birmingham. - 7.7.34

"Eastern Grandeur."

BIRMINGHAM
CENTENARY
CELEBRATIONS
1938
PAGEANT OF
BIRMINGHAM
ASTON PARK
11th to 16th JULY, 1938
PAGEANT MASTER - - *Gwen Lally*

King George V Silver Jubilee Party, Humpage Road, Bordesley, May 1935.

The Young People's Society celebrates the Coronation, Bournville, 1937.

Preparing to take part in a Summer Fete, 1938.

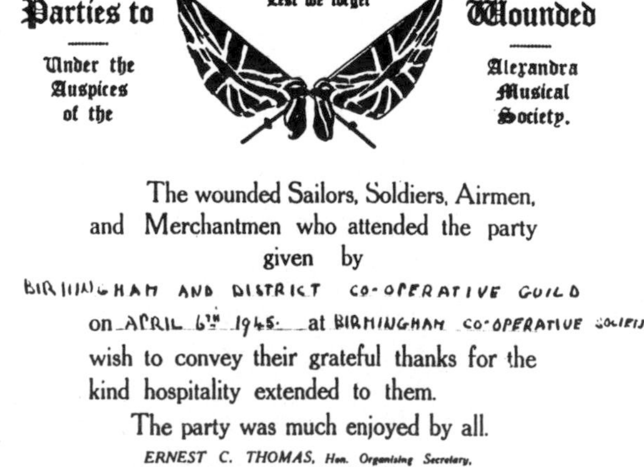

Parties to Wounded

Lest we forget

Under the Auspices of the Alexandra Musical Society.

The wounded Sailors, Soldiers, Airmen, and Merchantmen who attended the party given by BIRMINGHAM AND DISTRICT CO-OPERATIVE GUILD on APRIL 6th 1945 at BIRMINGHAM CO-OPERATIVE SOCIETY wish to convey their grateful thanks for the kind hospitality extended to them.

The party was much enjoyed by all.

ERNEST C. THOMAS, Hon. Organising Secretary, Alexandra Musical Society, 249, Albert Road, Aston, Birmingham, 6.

V.E. Party, Clay Lane, Yardley, May 1945.

"HOLIDAYS AT HOME"

16.8.45

TO-MORROW (FRIDAY)

12 noon to 9 p.m. — HANDSWORTH: Vegetable, Fruit & Flower Show.
3.0 & 6.45. — LIGHTWOODS: "THE ROOSTERS" Concert Party.
WARD END: "PLEASURE PIE" Concert Party.
3.0 & 6.0.—PERRY HALL and PYPE HAYES: Children's Entertainment.
6.0.—SMALL HEATH: Children's Entertainment.
6.45.—CANNON HILL: Kathleen Duncan's Radio and Variety Stars of 1945.
FUN FAIR at Handsworth Park.

Official Programmes on sale at Victoria Square Kiosk and at the Parks.

ILLUMINATED BUS AND TRAMCAR

TIMES AND ROUTES

As part of the victory celebrations in Birmingham an illuminated tramcar and omnibus will run on various routes. The vehicles will run on six evenings (Sunday excepted), beginning on "VE" Plus One Day.

On the first day, the tramcar will leave Kyotts Lake Road at 8.10 p.m. for Alcester Lanes End terminus, via Stratford Road, Moseley Road and Alcester Road, and will proceed later to Cannon Hill terminus for Navigation Street, then to Moseley Road via Leopold Street and back to Kyotts Lake Road.

On the second day it will leave Kyotts Lake Road at 7.40 p.m. for Stechford, proceed to Martineau Street via Bordesley Green, and afterwards take in routes serving Saltley and Alum Rock. Other routes will be covered on the subsequent evenings.

The illuminated omnibus will leave Kyotts Lake Road at 7.25 p.m. on the first day for Lincoln Road terminus via Warwick Road, and afterwards take in the Coventry Road, Yardley and Sheldon districts and the Outer Circle route.

On the second day it will leave Snow Hill at 7.30 p.m. for Hamstead, and will take in Walsall Road, Six Ways, Perry Common, Kingstanding, Pheasey Estate, Perry Barr, Summer Lane and various points of the City Circle bus route. Like the tramcar, the omnibus will cover other routes on the following days.

7.5.45

CITY OF BIRMINGHAM
—BATHS DEPARTMENT

BRIGHTER BIRMINGHAM, 1945

RE-OPENING OF ROWHEATH LIDO

At 7 p.m. TO-MORROW, Thursday, 17th May, the Right Worshipful Lord Mayor of Birmingham, Ald. W. T. Wiggins-Davies, J.P., will re-open

The LIDO AT ROWHEATH, BOURNVILLE

ADMISSION FREE.

On the opening night there will be a display of

TRICK and ORNAMENTAL SWIMMING

ON AND AFTER FRIDAY, 18th MAY, THE LIDO WILL BE OPEN FOR MIXED BATHING.

Mondays to Fridays ..	2 p.m.—9 p.m.
Saturdays	2 p.m.—8 p.m.
Sundays	11 p.m. 6 p.m.
Whit-Monday (only)	11 p.m.—6 p.m

A. J. PASHLER,
Acting General Manager and Secretary
Head Office: Kent Street, Birmingham 5
2nd May, 1945.

PAT COLLINS PRESENTS

LICKEY HILLS GREAT

WHIT VICTORY FAIR

AT THE FAIRGROUND, REDNAL

Commencing Saturday, May 19th, and Open Daily, Sundays included, until Sunday, May 27th.

ALL THE FUN OF THE FAIR

Smith's Imperial Coaches' annual outing for drivers – on a coach! Sparkbrook, 1948.

Birmingham holidaymakers, Dolphin Holiday Camp, Brixham, 1948.

Come and see the

ST. NEOTS QUADS

at our Stand at the

MOTHERCRAFT EXHIBITION

BINGLEY HALL · BIRMINGHAM

on Saturday

February 25th at 2p.m

These children were reared on —

COW & GATE MILK FOOD

The FOOD of ROYAL BABIES

1950

Newbridge Baptist Church Holiday in Ambleside, 1948.
They were all members of the Fellowship Holiday Association.

Announcing 1950

WINNERS

in the

KNITTING COMPETITION

organised by

SIRDAR WOOLS

in conjunction with

THE MOTHERCRAFT EXHIBITION

BIRMINGHAM

1st CLASS		2nd CLASS
Mrs. A. Cowdrill, 92, Tudor Street, Winson Green, BIRMINGHAM, 18.	20 GNS	Miss D. Birch, 8, Linden Lea, Finchfield, WOLVERHAMPTON.
L. E. Allen, 98, Alderbrook Road, Solihull, BIRMINGHAM.	10 GNS	Mrs. J. Smallwood, c/o 51, Wake Green Road, Moseley, BIRMINGHAM, 13.
Mrs. H. J. Neville, "Crathorne", Chapel Street, Chapel Terrace, Nr. WALSALL.	5 GNS	Mrs. H. L. Cemm, 25, Bankes Road, Small Heath, BIRMINGHAM. 10.

Yardley Old Church Youth Club members at Hilda Pritchett's 21st birthday party in the Trust School, Yardley, 1948.

14.7.52

6,500 at King's Norton Carnival

King's Norton carnival, at Cotteridge Park, on Saturday, was attended by 6,500 people. It was opened by the Lord Mayor of Birmingham (Ald W. T. Bowen), who urged the importance of Community Associations in the life of the city.

He appealed for more members for the associations so that events such as the carnival, to entertain and to provide funds for the furtherance of useful community activities, could prosper.

The Lady Mayoress was presented with a bouquet by Miss Barbara Barnes, of Dell Road, King's Norton, and with a basket of fruit by Miss Ann Grant, of King's Norton. The Lady Mayoress made presentations to the Carnival Queen, Miss June Anderton, of Midland Road, Cotteridge, and her four attendants.

25 Years' Carnivals

The carnival, which began with the hospital carnivals of 25 years ago, was revived in its present form in 1947 by Mr. W. Conway Cooper and Mr. E. J. Bartleet to increase interest in the newly-formed King's Norton Community Association, which now has 14 local associations affiliated to it—including an Over 50 Club, a horticultural society and a cycling club.

Cups for window dressing competitions were awarded to: George Masons (King's Norton area); Chadwin's Café (Stirchley area).

Carnival attractions were provided by the British Legion County Silver Band, Stirchley Physical Recreation Club, Billesley Arcadians, the Birmingham Scottish Pipe Band, St. Martin's in the Bull Ring Boys' Brigade (54th Birmingham Company) and members of Boys' Brigade South-west area of Birmingham.

The Atlas and Northern Assurance Companies' Annual Cricket Dinner, Market Hotel, Station Street, November 1949.

The Collins and Park families, of Selly Oak, take the Cliftonville air, 14th August 1951.

Father Christmas arrives at Colledge's newsagents, Baldwins Lane, Hall Green, c. 1949.

City of
BIRMINGHAM
Elizabeth R
1953
CORONATION
CELEBRATIONS
Official Programme

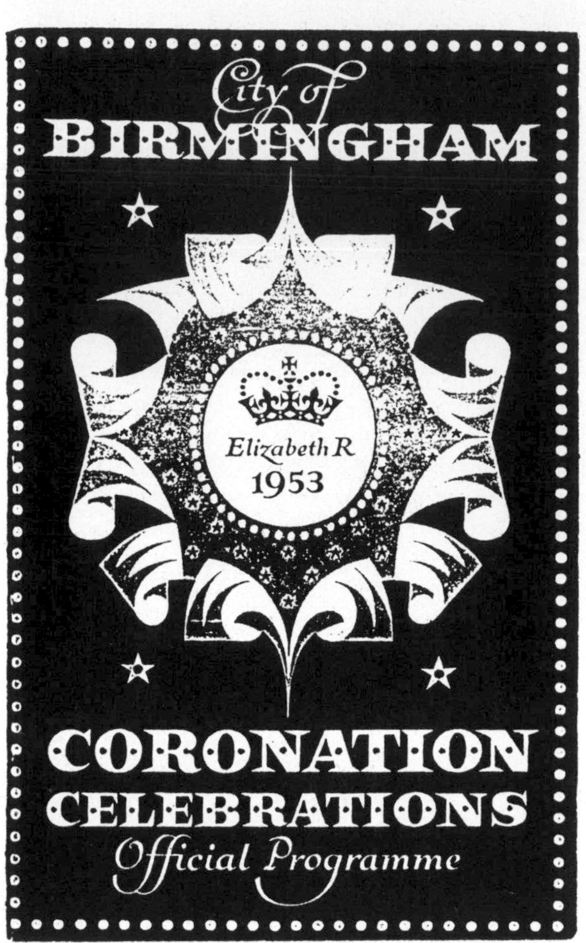

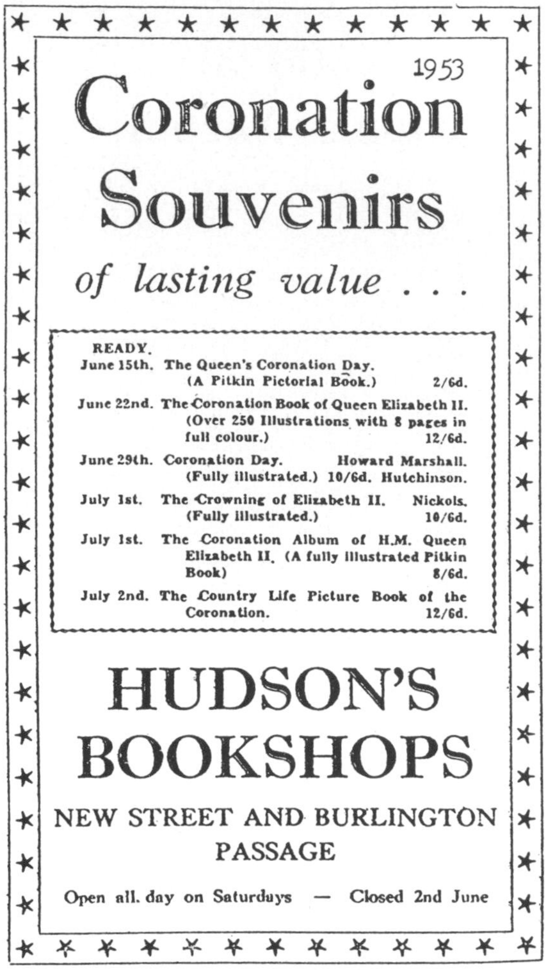
1953
Coronation
Souvenirs
of lasting value . . .
READY.
June 15th. The Queen's Coronation Day. (A Pitkin Pictorial Book.) 2/6d.
June 22nd. The Coronation Book of Queen Elizabeth II. (Over 250 Illustrations with 8 pages in full colour.) 12/6d.
June 29th. Coronation Day. Howard Marshall. (Fully illustrated.) 10/6d. Hutchinson.
July 1st. The Crowning of Elizabeth II. Nickols. (Fully illustrated.) 10/6d.
July 1st. The Coronation Album of H.M. Queen Elizabeth II. (A fully illustrated Pitkin Book) 8/6d.
July 2nd. The Country Life Picture Book of the Coronation. 12/6d.
HUDSON'S
BOOKSHOPS
NEW STREET AND BURLINGTON PASSAGE
Open all. day on Saturdays — Closed 2nd June

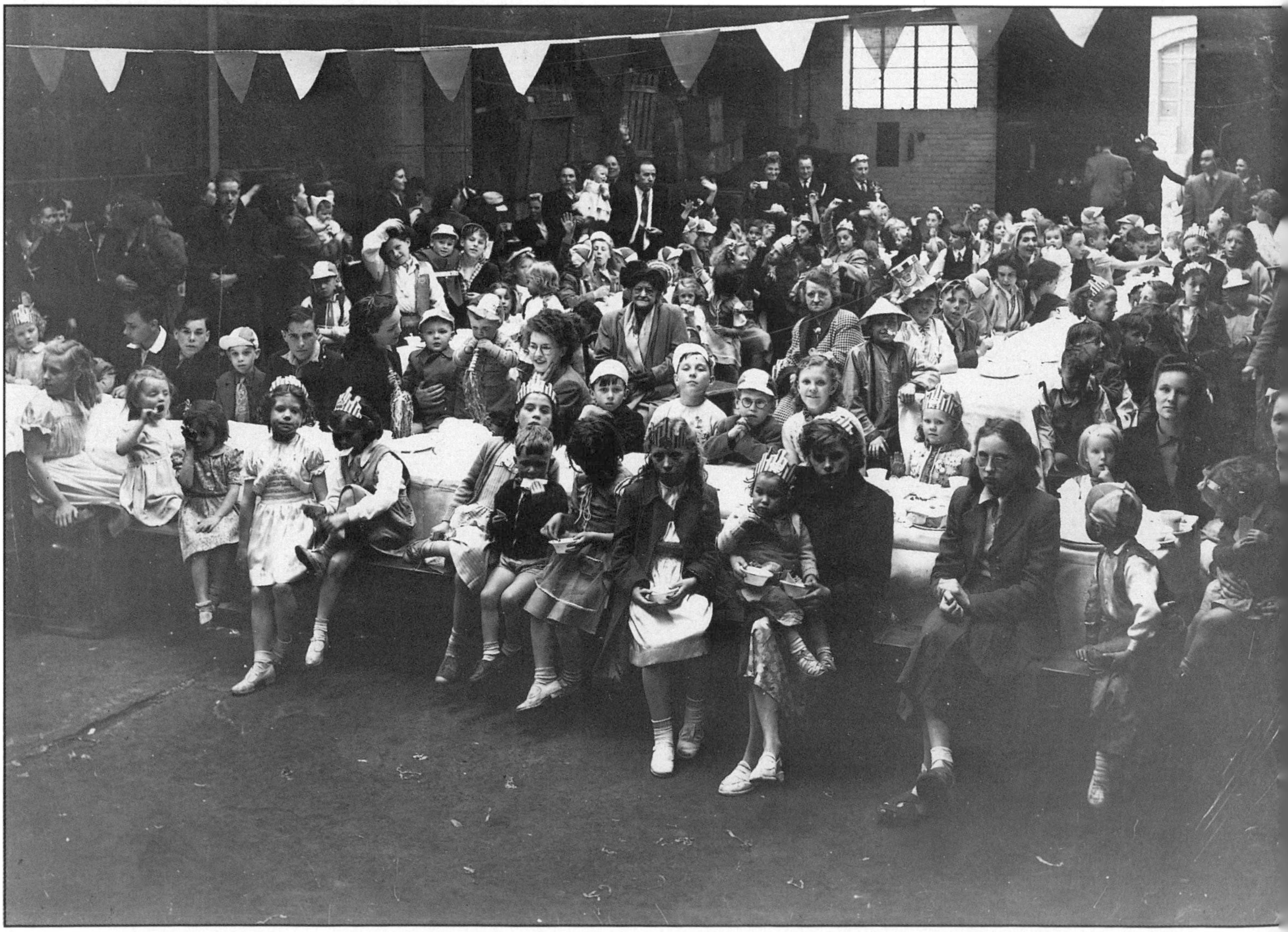

Balsall Heath residents' Coronation party, 1953.

St Mark's Street Coronation party,
Steward Street School, Spring Hill.

Bradstock Road and Dunster Close Coronation party, Kings Norton.

Coronation party, Broad Street
Presbyterian Church.

Coronation party for the residents of
Hollydale Road at Paget Road School, Erdington.

Dawberry Road Coronation group, Kings Heath.

Coronation party, Langstone Road, Warstock.

Christmas Day lunch, Royal Marines' Mess, HMS Birmingham, Hong Kong, 1954.

TONY HANCOCK, a young comedian who, 32 years before, was born on the Stratford Road, Hall Green, started a new series on BBC on July 6.

It was called "Hancocks Half Hour" and it was scheduled top run for six shows.

He topped the bill at the Birmingham Hippodrome a year later for the first time

Appearing with him were the Betty Fox dancers.

1956

IT WASN'T originally planned that way. But when the Queen came to Birmingham in November, 1955, she made sure she met the people.

And despite ceremonies at the Council House, King Edward's School, Edgbaston, and the new Gosta Green College of Technology, it was little Shard End that stole all the limelight.

Which must have delighted the Queen — just as it delighted the people of Shard End who turned out in the pouring rain to greet her.

She expressly asked to visit the suburb after she heard that the new Shard End church was being dedicated in the week of her visit.

At her request the arrangements for the Royal tour of the city were altered.

Cadbury Bros Ltd's General Office outing, Blackpool, c. 1955.

Garden Fete in St Laurence Rectory Garden Grounds, Northfield, 11th July 1959.

ATV star of "Tingha and Tucker", Jean Morton, brings the puppets to help her open the Amoco Service Station, Pershore Road South, Kings Norton, October 1964.

Birmingham Co operative Society Ltd., Butchery Dept., outing to the New Forest, c. 1960.

Birmingham Co-operative Society Ltd., Bakery Dept., outing to Symonds Yat, c. 1960.

KINGS HEATH HORSE SHOW SOCIETY

Annual

Dinner & Dance

FLORIDA ROOM

HOLTE HOTEL, ASTON

FRIDAY, 18th MARCH, 1966

President: P. E. Jull Esq., MBE

Birmingham Co-operative Society Ltd., Acocks Green Laundry Dept. outing, c. 1955.

THEATRICAL GARDEN PARTY

Under the auspices of the Birmingham Branch of The Actors' Church Union
President : The Rt. Rev. The Lord Bishop of Birmingham.
on **FRIDAY, JULY 1st, 1966, 3—6 p.m.**
at **ARDEN CROFT, SIR HARRY'S ROAD, EDGBASTON, BIRMINGHAM**
(by courtesy of Mr. and Mrs. W. Bushill-Matthews).
Tickets 5/- (including buffet) from Box Office, Birmingham Repertory Theatre.

Worthington coach trip to Killarney, 17th August 1967.

A promotional evening for the over-50's, given by Smith's Imperial Coaches of Sparkbrook, Solihull Civic Hall, October 1970.

Birmingham Zoo's two dromedaries, Arjan and Samantha, are crated up ready for the move to Cleethorpes Zoo, 4th May 1970. The Zoo, in Pershore Road, Edgbaston, was about to be converted into a pet's corner. Now it is known as the Birmingham Nature Centre.

BUMPER CROWDS IN PARK FOR GAY PROGRAMME

1970

BIRMINGHAM'S International Spring Festival at Cannon Hill Park is attracting bumper crowds, organisers said today.

Attendances had topped 45,000 mark and another 25,000 were expected today.

A spokesman for the Parks Department said: "Attendances so far are about double last year when we had the Tulip Festival, and the big rush day has yet to come—Spring Bank Holiday Monday."

This afternoon's events were starting with a rally of the Veteran Car Club of Great Britain.

About 50 cars were heading for Birmingham from all parts of the country to compete for the Parks Department commemorative plaque, being presented by the Lord Mayor, Alderman Stanley Bleyer.

The English Folk and Song Society were organising a folk dancing demonstration.

Arena shows were including sheepdog displays, band playing and battle demonstrations by the 3rd Battalion, Royal Green Jackets, who will also appear on Monday and Tuesday.

The soldiers were also giving a sky diving display over the park.

Tonight there will be international professional wrestling tournaments. Evening entertainment will close with a 15-minute firework display.

Zie Mister Jan Houwer, rare klompenmaker in a country noted for it, cannot start demonstrations of his craft in Birmingham until Thursday because there is a shortage of clogs in Holland.

One of only five manual clog makers in Holland, he has been kept at home in Aalten, near Arnhem, by pressures of work. So his son, Gerald, is setting up the clog-making show in Birmingham for the Tulip Festival at Cannon Hill Park. 1973

Susan Dale becomes the first Queen of Ladywood, at the Ladywood Community Centre Carnival, 15th September 1969.

Retirement Party for Maude Percy, Cadbury's Sales Accounts Office, c. 1972.

Contestants in the "Miss China" Beauty Contest, Smallbrook Ringway, 1974.

ATV presenter, Peter Tomlinson, congratulates the winner of the Jif Lemon Annual Pancake Race, Birmingham Bull Ring, February 1976.

Silver Jubilee celebrations, Clay Lane, Yardley, 7th June 1977.

Birmingham to London smooth as clockwork.

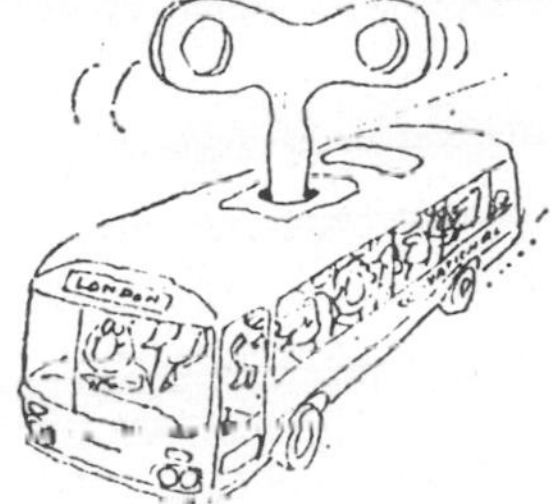

Every day - at 03·30, 06·30, 07·30, 08·30, 10·00, 12·00, 14·00, 16·00 and 18·30 – a shining white National Express Motorway coach leaves Digbeth coach station for London. And the period return fare is only £5·80.
Book your seat at National Travel, 65 Hurst Street, Birmingham or any Midland Red Travel office.

NATIONAL TRAVEL AGENT

National Express Coaches
GO OUR WAY–WE'RE GOING YOURS

NATIONAL

LYNEX LTD JOKES

COME AND SEE THE HORRORS!

We carry the largest range of jokes, joke novelties, magic, masks, hats and party sundries in Birmingham.
Also in stock – make-ups, disguises, theatrical props and fancy dress items

Come and see the specialists in fun at
167-169 MARY STREET
(Edward Road Corner)
DALSALL HEATH 1979
BIRMINGHAM B12 9RN
or call David Lynex on **021-440-1061**

UCTA
Birmingham Branch

UNITED COMMERCIAL TRAVELLERS ASSOCIATION (U.K.C.T.A.) INCORPORATED

CHAIRMAN'S
Dinner and Dance
THE BOTANICAL GARDENS, EDGBASTON
FRIDAY, 27th FEBRUARY, 1976

NATIONAL CHILDRENS HOME
Watson House, Watson Close, St. Bernards Rd.
Sutton Coldfield

GARDEN FETE

22nd May 1982 at 2.15 p.m.

Actress, Jane Rossington (left) of "Crossroads" fame, signs photographs for the members of the Perry Barr Bingo Club, Birchfield Road, 1982.

The girls, participating in the "Miss Europe" contest, practise their high kicks, Aston Hall, 1981.

1981

COACH HOLIDAYS
DIRECT FROM BIRMINGHAM DIGBETH COACH STATION

Terrific value for money, compare our prices first

8 DAYS - ISLE OF WIGHT
SANDOWN - HALF BOARD

July 11, 18 .... £99
July 25, Aug. 1, 8 ..... £102
Aug. 15, 22, 29 ...... £102
Sept. 5, 12, 19 .... £93

8 DAYS - ISLE OF WIGHT
SHANKLIN - HALF BOARD

July 11 .... £86
July 18, 25 .... £93
Aug. 1, 8, 15, 22 ...... £93
Aug. 29 .... £86
Sept. 5, 12, 19, 26 ..... £86

8 DAYS - CLIFTONVILLE
FULL BOARD

October 3, 10 .... £54
October 17, 24 .... £51

8 DAYS - EASTBOURNE
HALF BOARD

July 11 .... £87
July 18, 25 .... £90
August 1, 8, 15 .... £90
August 22, 29 .... £87
September 5, 12 ...... £87
September 19, 26 ..... £83
October 3 .... £72
October 10 .... £69
October 17 .... £65

8 DAYS - TORQUAY
HALF BOARD

June 13, 20 .... £84
July 11 .... £95
August 15, 22, 29 ..... £95
September 5 .... £84
Sept. 12, 19, 26 .... £74
October 3, 10 .... £72
October 17, 24 .... £69

Extras: Single Rooms
Insurance £3.75

BOOK NOW ONLY AT

LEWIS'S
TRAVEL BUREAU
BULL STREET, BIRMINGHAM B4 6AQ
Tel: 021-236 7611

Access, Barclaycard and telephone bookings welcome

Students give a French flavour to the annual rag procession, 17th November 1984.

UNIVERSITY OF BIRMINGHAM - CHEMICAL ENGINEERING SOCIETY

The Chemical Engineering Society invites you to their

Thirty-seventh Annual Dinner

on Wednesday, 8th February 1984.
at The Grand Hotel (Via Barwick Street), Birmingham.
commencing with a sherry Reception at 7.00 p.m.

R.S.V.P.
Head of Department's Secretary,
Department of Chemical Engineering,
University of Birmingham,
Birmingham, B15 2TT

Undergraduate Chairman:
Richard Aston

CANCER RESEARCH CAMPAIGN
(Warley Committee)

Present their

V. E. DAY CELEBRATION
DINNER AND DANCE

on

WEDNESDAY 8th MAY 1985

at

THE GRAND HOTEL, BIRMINGHAM

Dancing to the

JOE LOSS ORCHESTRA

1945 - 1985 40 YEARS OF PEACE

ELECTRICAL CONTRACTORS' ASSOCIATION

Mercia Branch

Ladies' Evening

Annual

Dinner and Dance

Dorchester Suite, Penns Hall Hotel
Sutton Coldfield

FRIDAY 18th OCTOBER 1985

Chairman
Mr. A. J. E. HARPER

West Midlands Fire Service

Officers Club

DINE IN

With
Celebrity Speaker

Thursday 26th April 1990
Fire Service Headquarters

The Four Oaks Club
AUTUMN DINNER

SATURDAY 11th OCTOBER 1986

IT'S ALL IN THE GAME

SYDNEY 1879. MELBOURNE 1880.

IMPORTANT NOTICE.

THOS. SMITH & SONS,

THE FOUNDERS OF THE BICYCLE & TRICYCLE INDUSTRIES, CONTINUE TO SUPPLY

FITTINGS & EVERY REQUISITE

FOR

BICYCLE MAKERS & RIDERS.

The success which attended our Sydney Exhibits, where we gained a Silver Medal, has in spite of all competition been continued at Melbourne, where we have gained the Highest Award for excellence of Workmanship and Finish of our BICYCLE FITTINGS and MATERIALS.

1882

FOR

BICYCLES & TRICYCLES

The Cheapest and Soundest Built Machines in the Market, apply to

THOMAS SMITH & SONS,

SALTLEY MILL, ADDERLEY ROAD, BIRMINGHAM.

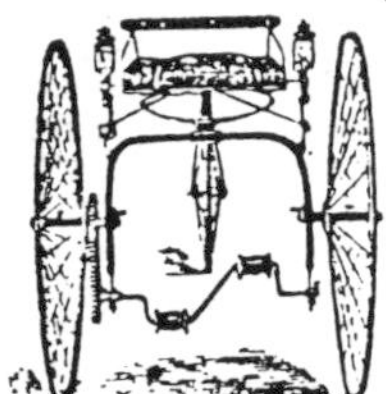

PATENTEES,
The ORIGINAL BICYCLE STAMPERS and FORGERS, and Manufacturers of all Bicyclists' and Tricyclists' FITTINGS & REQUISITES.
Makers of the celebrated

EMPRESS TRICYCLE

SADDLES OF EVERY MAKE AND STYLE.

Sole Licensees of the "Wicksteed" Bicycle Stand.

SATCHELS AND POCKETS IN GREAT VARIETY.

TESTIMONIALS FROM ALL PARTS OF THE WORLD.

Larry Burns and his genial friend and adviser, Pat Moran, have left Birmingham, in which city they have made a whole host of friends. Each will carry with him any amount of good wishes, and, should they return, they can rest assured of a hearty welcome.

* * *

Mr. Fred Jones, who presides over the Clements' Vaults, Newtown Row, Birmingham, is a valuable addition to the list of vocalists on the programme of smoking concerts. I hear that his services have been received by the choirmaster of a church in the neighbourhood.

* * *

Anthony Diamond has secured the services of Jabez White, Charley Simpson, and Harry Tongue as assistants. His boxing academy at the rear of the "Green Lamp," Dale End, Birmingham, is being largely supported, and some likely lads will shortly emerge from Anthony's stable.

* * *

The members of the Olympic Club are disappointed that there is no likelihood of a second match between Harry Greenfield and Larry Burns taking place in Birmingham. The young American has gained a host of friends during his stay in Birmingham, and he would have no difficulty in securing a substantial backing for a second trial against the Camden Town man. Charley Tilley is also red-hot on the trail of the latter, who, however, appears to be content to rest for a while on the laurels he recently won by beating Burns.

* * *

The desire to accord Mr. Jack Brown, of Birmingham, a testimonial, is almost unanimous in the Midlands. Mr. Brown is one of the oldest supporters of the prize ring, and could be found in the corners of most of the fighters from Brum, when "things was things," to quote the expression of this great old sport. I have been deputed to look up a suitable place for the "ben" and was lucky enough to run across Mr. Harry Lyons, the genial manager of the Queen's Theatre, at the Olympic Club the other night who expressed his willingness to assist the movement in any way. A list of donations in aid of the movement has been opened; I shall be pleased to receive and acknowledge amounts, large or small, and cannot too strongly urge the claims of "one of the best" to the notice of those who admire one of the bull-dog breed who has fallen upon rough times.

1897

INDOOR GAMES.	GOLFING.	MECHANICAL TOYS.
Playing Cards	Golf Clubs	Clockwork Trains
Backgammon	Golf Balls	Steam Boats
Drawbridge	Golf Bags	Electric Trains
Ring Quoits	Golf Gloves	Fire Boats
Draughts	**TENNIS.**	Clockwork Boats
Dominoes	Tennis Rackets	Motor Cars
Bezique	Tennis Presses	Submarine Boats
Bridge	Tennis Sets	Stations
Picuet	Tennis Bags	Railway Engines
Poker	Tennis Boots	Bridges
Whist	**CRICKET.**	Turbine Engines
Chess	Cricket Bats	Ticket Sets
Ascot	Cricket Balls	Hot-air Engines
Sandown	Cricket Stumps	Tunnels
Puzzles	Batting Gloves	Electric Lamps
Rouiette	Gauntlets	Signals
Wibly Wob	Leg Guards	Crossing Gates
Table Hockey	Cricket Bags	Meccano
Table Cricket		Working Models
Table Football		Railway Cars
Table Croquet		Steam Engines
		Luggage Trucks

FOOTBALL.	BADMINTON.	HOCKEY.
Football Boots	Badminton Rackets	Hockey Sticks
Footballs	Badminton Sets	Hockey Shoes
Football Bags	Badminton Poles	Hockey Balls
Football Jerseys	Badminton Nets	Hockey Bags
Club Colours	Shuttlecocks	Hockey Shirts
Shin Guards	Boxing Gloves	Hockey Gloves
Football Knickers	Punching Balls	Shin Guards
Boys' Footballs	Exercisers	Hockey Knicks

SPECIAL MINIATURE BILLIARD TABLE for £5 19 6

Size 6ft. × 3ft., Slate Bed, Best Cloth, Low Rubber Cushions, Six Pockets Solid Mahogany Frame, Detachable Screw Legs, Cues, Marking Board, and 3 Ivory Balls—Carriage Paid within twenty miles

$10\frac{1}{2}$D. ST. GEORGE $10\frac{1}{2}$D.
GOLF BALLS,
10/6 PER DOZEN.

TESTIMONIAL.

Edgbaston, November 28th, 1908.

Dear Sir,—I am greatly obliged to you for letting me have a dozen of your Grenville St. George Balls so promptly. I have used all kinds of balls in the past years, but at present I can find no fault with your ball at 10½d. as compared with Kites, Elerts, Colonels, etc. They are first rate off the irons, and absolutely right off the wooden clubs.

There may be something wrong about them, but I, a middle handicap man, have not found it yet. The first time I used one—a gift—I went out in 37. To-day I won the medal with one—played 36 holes with it—and it is as good as new. I distributed several. I only hope you will keep up the quality and keep down the price.

Please send me two dozen more. I enclose cheque.

Yours, (Signed).

2/9 ST. GEORGE 2/9
GOLF CLUBS.

BRASSIES, DRIVERS, CLEEKS, IRONS, LOFTING CLUBS, MASHIES, NIBLICKS, PUTTERS, SAMMIES - - JIGGERS. First Quality, in all shapes, - -

3/6 each, Special 2 9. 1908

GRENVILLE'S

12, Cherry Street,

Opposite Cobden Hotel.

REMOVED FROM CORPORATION ST

Handsworth Tennis Club, 1894.

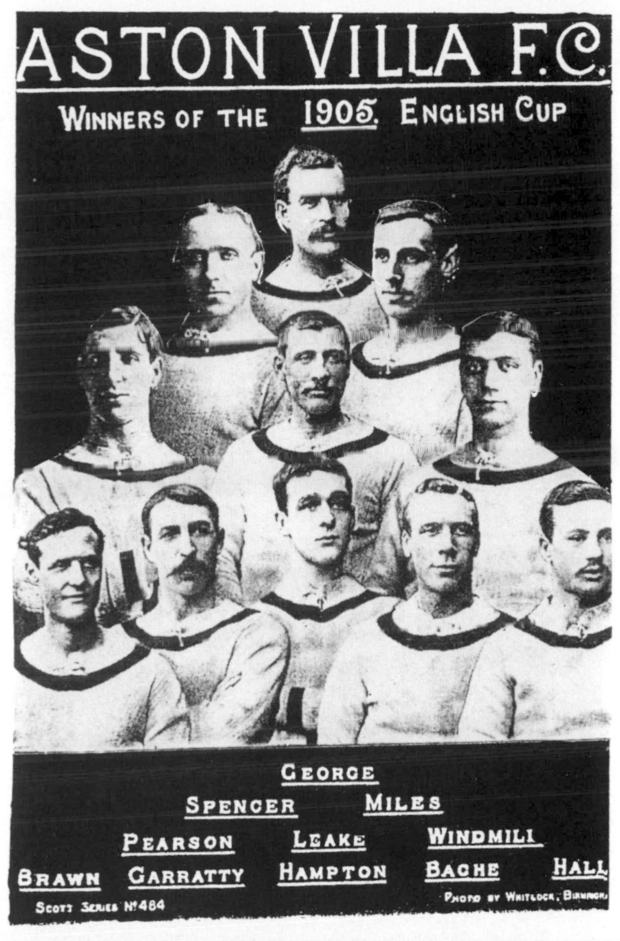

A.G. Spalding & Bros., (athletic goods), 57 New Street, 1909.

Do you recognise the handsome captain of this group of footballers? He is George Robey (seated second from the left), complete with eyebrows, who skippered a team of famous players (shown above) against Aston Villa at Villa Park in February 1910. He was a talented amateur footballer in his day. The other figures (left to right) are:—Standing: T. Horne (Oxford City) (referee), W. C. Athersmith (Small Heath), Cooch (Aston Villa), Frank Forman (Nottingham Forest), J. Jones (Wolverhampton Wanderers), J. Iremonger (Nottingham Forest), J. Holford (Stoke), J. Carlin (trainer). Seated: Vivian J. Woodward (Tottenham Hotspur), Leonard (Small Heath), E. Needham (Sheffield United). Seat on his heels: Lockett (Stoke).

EDGBASTON RESERVOIR SKATING RINK.

New and Enlarged Rink. New Floor.
New Ball-Bearing Skates.
NOW OPEN.
Three Sessions Daily.: 10 to 12.30, 2.30 to 5, and 7 to 10.
BAND of the ROYAL STAFFORDSHIRE BLUES (Bandmaster, A. Roberts), Every Afternoon and Evening.
Tuition: Morning and Afternoon Sessions.

BILLIARDS. 1909

TWENTY-FOUR "PADMORE" TABLES
AT
PRINCE'S CAFE,
CORPORATION STREET (New Street end),
AND
CARLTON CAFE,
FORE STREET
CORPORATION STREET (New Street end).

Lozells' Cycling Club, 1908.

THE LOZELLS SKATING RINK

A novel feature has been introduced in connection with the Lozells Skating Rink, and thus for the convenience of business people, viz., an early morning session from 6 to 8 a.m. This will give many an opportunity which they would not otherwise have of indulging in this popular and healthful recreation. 15.5.09

Birmingham Walking Club about to set off from Birmingham City F.C. Ground to Coventry, New Year's Day 1911. The Bishop of Birmingham, Dr Russell Wakefield, stands (right) with starting pistol at the ready.

Handsworth Swimming Club, Grove Lane Baths, c. 1913.

Queslett F.C., Hamstead, 1921.

Kings Norton Senior Schools' Football Association Team, Northfield Road, 1927/8.

B.S.A.—The Motor Cycles of Proved performance and value

Success after success gained in open competition—and consistently reliable everyday service in the hands of riders like yourself—these are undeniable proof of B.S.A. performance and value. Solo from £37 10s. With sidecar from £57 5s. Or on Hire-Purchase Terms.

CALL OR SEND FOR LATEST CATALOGUE.

DE LUXE MODEL

Car comfort for £4 Tax

B.S.A. Three Wheelers

Front wheel drive, three speeds and reverse, all-wheel braking, quickly detachable and interchangeable wheels, electric starter, car-type controls, and 9-h.p. engine and £4 tax—these are some of the features of B.S.A Three Wheelers. Three models—De Luxe and Sports (2 seaters) both £100. Family (seating 2 adults and 2 children) £105.

NOW ONLY £100

TRIAL RUNS WITH PLEASURE: EXCHANGES.

County Cycle & Motor Co. Ltd.

300-301, Broad St., Birmingham

Repair Dept.: 164-8, BATH ROW

QUAIFE'S

CRICKET BATS from 10/6 each.

CRICKETBALLS from 6/6 each.

ALL GOODS AT LOWEST PRICES.

Illustrated Cricket, Tennis and Bowls Catalogues. Post Free. SPECIAL TERMS.

318, Broad St., Birmingham

Winners of the Kings Norton Swimming Championship, 1927/8.

Sparkhill Youth F.C., c. 1927.

BY THE WAY.

By Beachcomber.

A DESPAIRING angler writes to tell me that he cannot catch any fish.

He must remember that fish are not prepared to flock round his feet for the mere fun of being jabbed through the jaw with a hook. The free meal is no sufficient inducement.

Which of us would accept an invitation to lunch if we suspected that, at a signal, the host or hostess would rise and transfix us with a rusty spear?

* * *

Poor Fish.

The fish must be tamed gradually. They must be given the food without the hook. Then, one day, when they are eating at their ease, all unsuspicious of the rod of Damocles above their heads, jab! Thirty-nine tiny teeth bite on the hard steel! Hold him, sir! And so another toiler of the deep or marine fool has paid the supreme penalty, and passed to that bourne whence no fish returns.

None of which applies to whales, cuttle-fish, minnows or novelists.

MITCHELLS & BUTLERS

FOOTBALLERS'

GRILL ROOMS,

OPEN TILL 10 P.M.

EXCHANGE RESTAURANT STEPHENSON PLACE. Telephone—Midland 1027, 0751	THE WHITE HORSE CONGREVE STREET. Telephone—Central 6146, 6147
OLD ROYAL RESTAURANT TEMPLE ROW. Telephone—Central 5403, 3492	CROWN HOTEL CORPORATION STREET. Telephone—Central 1388

SPECIAL TERMS TO CLUBS. *Apply to the Managers.*

MOLE & WOOD, LTD.

We specialise in all

HARD TENNIS COURT & GARDEN Requisites

Quarries: Great Barr & Hamstead

64, COLESHILL ST. BIRMINGHAM

Dial ASTON X, 2611-2

St Barnabus Gym Club, Ladywood, c. 1928.

THE GOLF SHOE DE LUXE

Number 774

"Lotus" Model

GUARANTEED WATERPROOF.

You can buy this shoe and a fine range suitable for all purposes, Ladies' and Gents' wear, at the store which has built up its reputation on Quality Footwear.

A few of our Specialities :—
" LOTUS," " DELTA," " NORVIC,"
" MASCOT," ∴ " PORTLAND,"
" HEALTH," " SWAN," etc., etc.

J. Cleland & Son

79, Hamstead Road,
HANDSWORTH

'PHONE NORTHN. 398, and we will collect your repairs, for which we have the same quality reputation.

THRILLS BY THE SCORE!

Neck-to-Neck Racing in Pairs

AT

LILLESHALL

On Wolverhampton to Newport Road,
(14 miles) (3 miles)

ON

Whit-Saturday, May 26th, 1928

COMMENCING AT THREE P.M.

SPEED TRIALS

For Motor Cycles, Solo and Sidecar Machines, Three-wheeled Cycle Cars and Cars, organised by the BIRMINGHAM MOTOR CYCLE CLUB.

Many Valuable Trophies to be Competed for.

The First Event of its kind at Lilleshall.
"A MINIATURE T.T."

BOOK THE DATE and be EARLY

First man away at 3 p.m. prompt.

Further details may be obtained from the Secretary, Birmingham Motor Cycle Club, 181, May Lane, Kings Heath, Birmingham.
'Phone : Warstock 96.

White Rovers F.C., Stirchley, 1935/6.

THIS WILL INTEREST YOU !

1932

GUILDHOUSE

Oozells Street North

ADULT SCHOOL MEETING

Every Sunday Morning at 10-0

Every week-night the Social Club provides facilities for Billiards, Table Tennis, etc. We have plans to further extend our social activities, but badly need more members. . .

COME AND JOIN US, YOU WILL BE MADE WELCOME

CAN JOIN

THE LUCAS SPORTS CLUB

FOR ONLY

ONE PENNY

PER WEEK

Details from the Sports' Office

JOIN NOW!

1935

POINTS WIN FOR ALF. PASS

Winner's Superior Left-Hand Work

10.12.36

DESPITE the fact that owing to a breakdown in transit caused by the fog, which prevented one of the contests taking place, the Imperial Amateur Boxing Club carried through a good programme last night.

In the main event, a bout at catch-weights, A. Pass (Imperial) beat A. Edwards (Guest, Keen and Nettlefolds) on points over six rounds.

Pass, although fully extended throughout, owed his success—he conceded a good deal of weight—to his superiority in the infighting passages during the first half of the fight.

BRUM "BOGY" AT BLACKBURN.

1935

THE Ewood plot has thickened. After the League game between Blackburn Rovers and Birmingham a fortnight ago most people outside Birmingham felt pretty sure the Rovers would win the cup-tie. Birmingham had scoring chances which they did not take but over the ninety minutes the Rovers looked the better team.

Then came the Brums' clear-cut win over the Arsenal last Saturday. This was the biggest beating the Arsenal have had all the season. It was Birmingham's best display all season. The cup-tie doesn't look such a good thing for Blackburn now.

A CLEAN SHEET.

I am forgetting about the League game. Look at the teams. Men, not memories, count. The Rovers do not impress me a lot. Jack Hughes has done well in place of Cliff Binns, the first-choice goalie. I will say that the Rovers have not conceded a goal in their three cup games but the backs do not always look safe and sound.

Walter Crooks is a promising subject here but a cup game like this is a big test for a young lad.

In the Rovers' middle line Arnold Whiteside stands out for constructive touches. Norman Christie and Bob Pryde are better defenders.

The danger men in the attack are the wingers. Jack Bruton is an awkward player to tackle. He keeps the ball close and referees often make a whistling noise when Jack is brought down. Over on the left Jackie Milne is popping up with goals that count.

At inside-forward, though, the Rovers are not so striking. Tom McLean is wily but not a shot. Beattie, playing centre-forward, is strong but, like Talbot, the inside-right, is not subtle.

A SPLENDID DEFENCE.

Birmingham are right in one cup-tie requirement. They have a defence bettered by few. Hibbs, Booton and Barkas are the names. The left-back didn't play in the League game. Compared with that day the Brums will be stronger all round.

Especially will this be so in attack, where Blackburn's Birmingham "bogy" will make his bow. This is Joe Bradford. Joe has a great record as Ewood Park. Besides his own scoring possibilities, too, Joe knows the passes to give Wilson Jones, a very clever centre-forward. The other forwards, White, Harris and Guest have all improved with first team experience.

I fancy Birmingham will be a different team to what they were in the recent League game. In spite of that result, or perhaps because of it, I fancy the Midlanders more than a little. Their strong defence looks enough to hold the Rovers' attack. Brimingham should at least get a draw.

"WHO WAS SHE?"

TO THE EDITOR OF THE BIRMINGHAM POST

Sir,—The letters under the above heading have interested me very much, as my wife started bicycling in 1891 or 1892, and a girl cousin earlier still. We heard some amusing remarks, such as: "Eh! a lady of a wench on a bicycle"; "The lady will beat you, old man"; and in one village an elderly lady stood still, gazed and then remarked: "Well, I *like* that." There were no really rude remarks, but my wife wore a short skirt, which was a nuisance at times.

W. M. BAKER.

"Woodeaves," 58, Middleton Hall Road, King's Norton, September 15.

19/9/38

SOUTH BIRMINGHAM MOTOR CLUB

GYMKHANA

Saturday, August 22nd, 1936

at 3 p.m.

IN FIELDS ADJOINING HEADQUARTERS AT

THE MALT SHOVEL, BARSTON

Near Hampton-in-Arden.

EVENTS OPEN TO ALL MOTOR CYCLISTS.

Admission by Programme 6d. **Free Parking**

All entries for events to be made on Ground.

SLOW RACE; READING RACE; MUSICAL CHAIRS; BALL and BUCKET RACE; OBSTACLE RACE; TENT PEGGING; TURF RIDING, etc., etc.,

EVENTS FOR CAR OWNERS.

THE question of admission prices to Birmingham League games has again arisen as a result of Cannock Town's decision to reduce the charge from one shilling to sixpence.

It was raised to one shilling before the season opened as an experiment. Apparently this has not succeeded.

THE Birmingham League enforces no ruling upon its clubs with regard to admission with the exception that the minimum shall be sixpence, boys excepted.

This is a wise plan for the circumstances of clubs in the Birmingham League greatly vary.

Almost without exception the Midland clubs in the Birmingham League charge sixpence. It is all a question of proximity to the League sides.

When a Birmingham League side's ground is situated less than ten miles from that of a First or Second Division club, it would be unwise to charge any higher price for admission.

Clubs a little further away from Birmingham, such as Kidderminster and Worcester, have fixed a rate of ninepence.

The Shropshire and North Wales clubs and Hereford United, all of whom are too far away from big football centres for thei rattendances to be appreciably affected, can draw a shilling gate without affecting their attendance figures.

The fog and bad weather "bogey" begins to raise its head at this time of the year, and attendances are bound to suffer.

Even more annoying are abandoned and cancelled matches. Oakengates and Colwyn Bay suffered on Saturday.

10.12.36

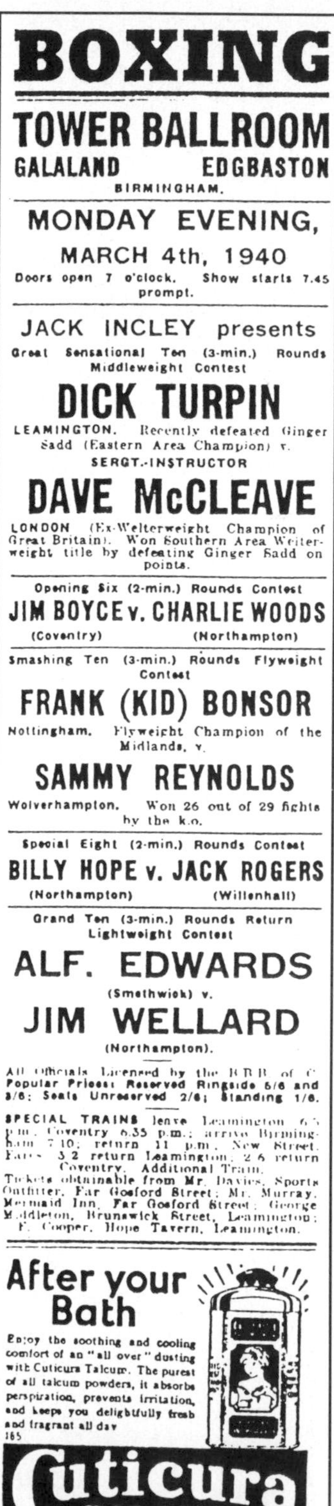

WATER POLO TROPHIES PRESENTED 1936

There was a large attendance of water polo enthusiasts at the annual dinner and distribution of trophies at the Star Vaults, Birmingham.

The President, Mr. J. E. Reynolds, handed the trophies to the successful clubs. The winners were: Water polo: First Division, Coventry S. and L.S.S.: Second Division, Smethwick S.C.; Third Division, Small Heath and Harriers; Fourth Division, Summerfield S.C.

In the Third and Fourth Divisions Small Heath and Summerfield respectively went through the season without a defeat.

Team Race Championship. — First Division, Coventry S. and L.S.S.; Second Division, Wolverhampton; Third Division, Westminster Handsworth; Fourth Division, Boldmere S.C.

Canning Shield Competition.—Coventry S. and L.S.S.

Mention was also made of the fact that for the first time the Birmingham League had defeated the London League and league badges were presented to the members of the Birmingham League side: J. Carter (Aston), T. Barratt (Coventry), W. R. Dickson (Stafford), G. Leach (Aston), C. H. Dumbledon (Stafford), A. R. Wood and J. Kelway (Coventry).

BENNY FISHER TO RETIRE FROM RING

5. 11. 40

BENNY FISHER, of Austin B.C., winner of a string of Midland amateur boxing titles, has decided to retire from the ring.

Fisher, winner of over 90 per cent. of the 325 contests he has fought, is engaged on war work and finds little time for training.

One of the most brilliant amateur fly-weights the Midlands has produced, he was unlucky not to win a National title in 1938.

In that year he lost the title on a casting vote when A. Russell, of Rotherham, was awarded the decision after a thrilling final.

During his schooldays Fisher was virtually a cripple. An operation for knee trouble followed by many weeks in hospital, made him fit to walk again.

His left leg is a shade smaller than his right, but Fisher overcame this handicap.

He was told to get plenty of exercise. Boxing interested him and he soon became a useful exponent.

Brilliant start

He won three championships in his first year of boxing, when he was barely 15.

A product of the Birmingham Union of Boys' Clubs, he won their 6st. and 6st. 7lb. titles in 1930. He also won the Birmingham J.O.C. 6st. 7lb. title in the same year.

When he joined the senior ranks he quickly made his mark. He had not been out of a Midland fly-weight final since 1934 Last May he won the championship for the fourth time.

In 1938 he brought off a double by winning the fly and bantam-weight titles.

He represented England several times and figured in Midland A.B.A. teams in representative matches for some years.

Unaware that war was about to break out that very day, ramblers from Bournville Parish Church Youth Club prepare to set out, 3rd September 1939.

Post Office Sports' Day, Fordrough Lane, Bordesley Green, 3rd July 1937.

Chamberlain & Hookham Sports' Day, Common Lane, Sheldon, 26th June 1937.

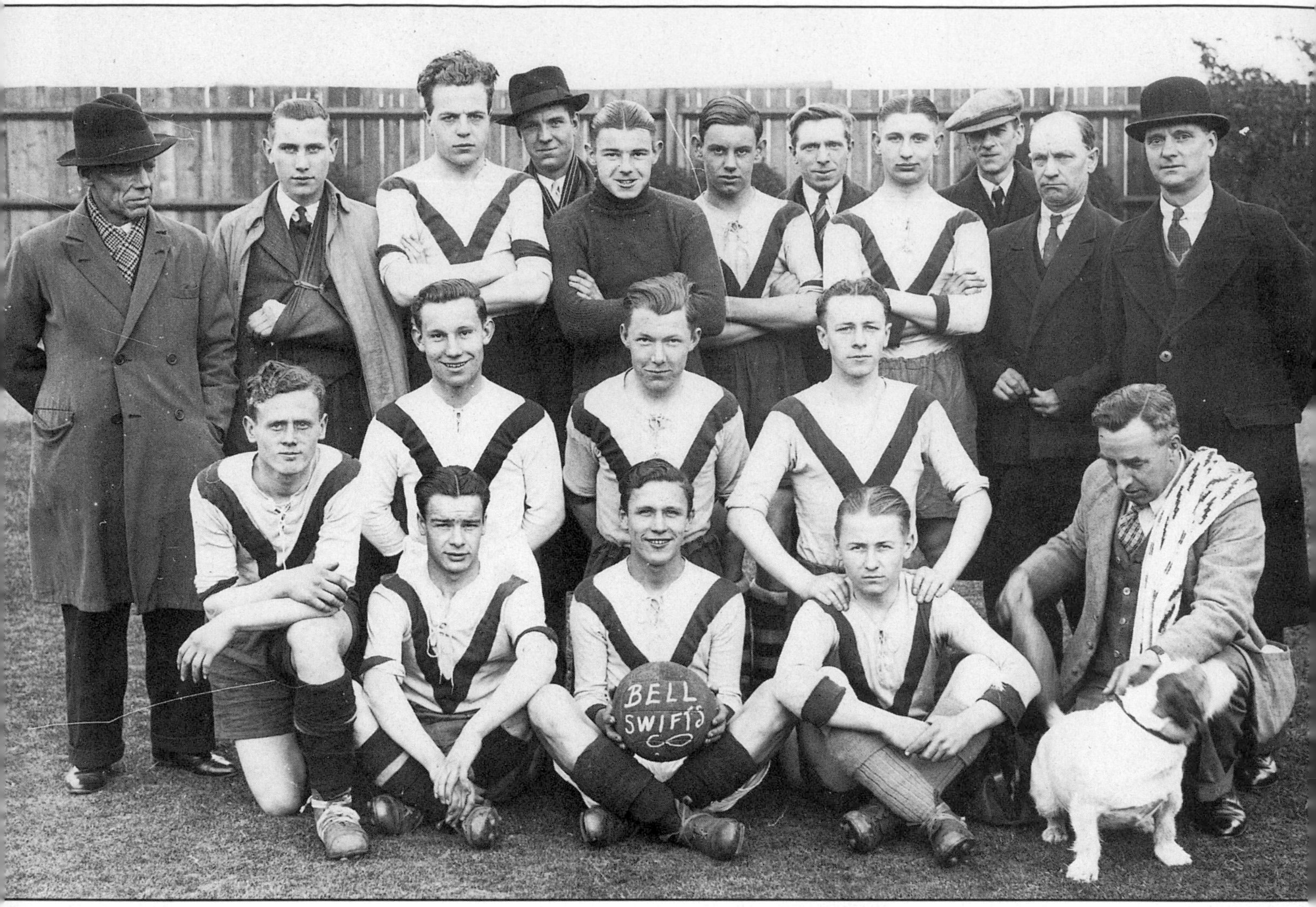

Bell Swifts F.C., Northfield, 1937.

KNOCKOUT BARGAINS - WINDSCREENS - LEGSHIELDS - TOOLS

CABLES - HEADLAMPS - PETROL TANKS

HELMETS - GLOVES - SADDLES - DUALSEATS - CARRIERS - MUDGUARDS

FRAMES AND SIDECAR CHASSIS - WHEELS

NOW COME AND SEE OUR SHOW

at

THE ROCKER BOX

110-112 ASTON ROAD, BIRMINGHAM 6

(Between Dartmouth Street and Hubert Street)

Cut Price Motorcycle and Scooter Accessories

Try us first and save yourself money

Place Your Racing and Greyhound Pools Investments

WITH

MARTINEAU POOLS

AND YOUR

Racing and Greyhound Bets

At S.P. or TOTE ODDS with

SAFFER & SON,

BURLINGTON CHAMBERS,

118, NEW STREET, BIRMINGHAM

WRITE FOR PARTICULARS OF ALL EVENTS

Telephones: MID. 5555 and 6, and MID. 5881 and 2

JACK WOOLF Ltd (FOOTBALL POOLS)

NOW FOR OUR

JOCKEY POOLS

THE EASY COUPON WHICH PAYS THE

BIG DIVIDENDS

SEND 6d. FOR A SUPPLY OF COUPONS TO

P.O.: BOX No. 88, SMALLBROOK STREET, BIRMINGHAM

THE SPORTING COUPON FOR SPORTSMEN

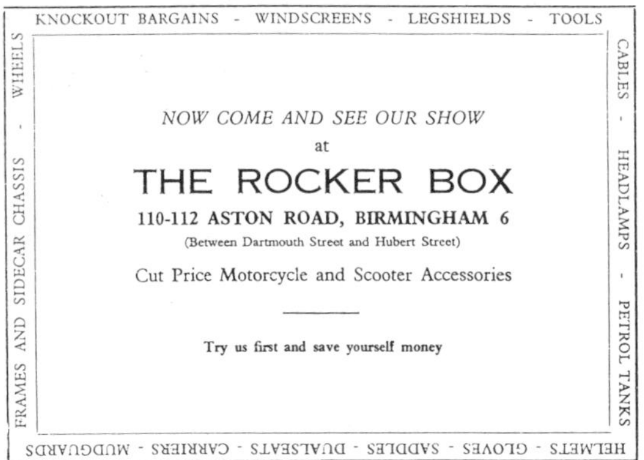

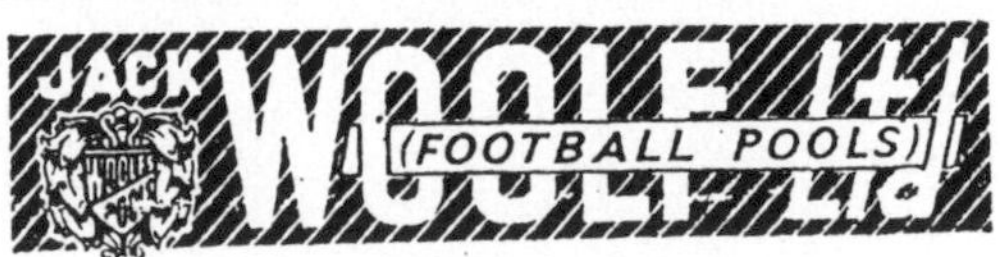

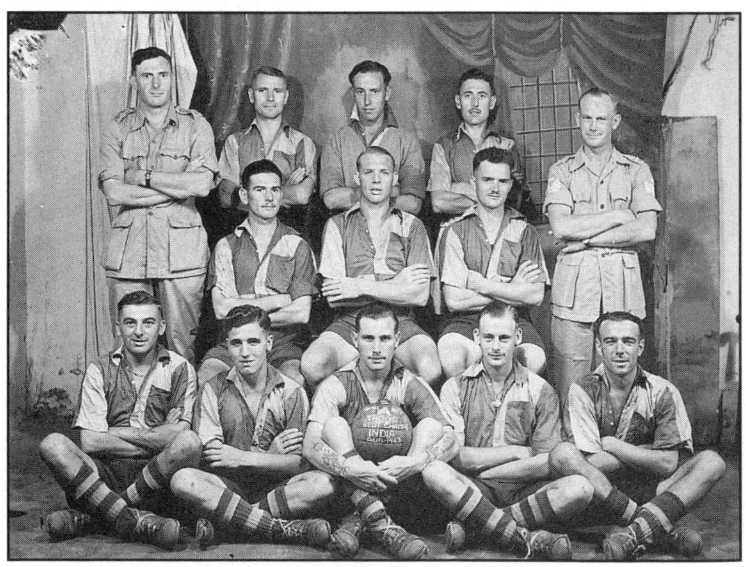

122nd Anti-tank Regiment football team (mainly comprised of Birmingham soldiers, recruited at Thorp Street), India, 1943.

SIR,—Here in Birmingham we have two fine parks, Small Heath and Cannon Hill, with boating pools, bowling greens, tennis courts, and swimming pools, but on the one free day (Sunday) which the majority of workers have for recreation, they are debarred from enjoying these amenities owing to the fact that in the far dim past a restriction was imposed, though whether objecting to amusement or recreation is not quite clear.

Recreation is healthy exercise and should be allowed. We are asked to restrict travel, but the residents of these districts have to travel if they wish to avail themselves of various forms of exercise.

JUNE 1944

ONLY 5 MATCHES IN BRUM TENNIS

After obtaining leave from his unit and travelling from Peterborough to Birmingham to play in the Priory Club Whitsun Tennis Tournament yesterday, J. E. Rudd, a corporal in the Green Howards, found he was drawn against Jack Harper, the Australian, in his first game in the open singles—and Harper was in Manchester playing against Britain.

The Australian will not play in Birmingham before Tuesday, and until he arrives Rudd will compete in two other events.

After only five matches had been played in the first round of the women's open singles, rain caused an abandonment. Results:

Miss P. Fisher beat Miss S. Hill 6—2, 6—1; Miss D. M. Litherland beat Miss M. Evans 6—3, 6—0; Miss M. Osborne beat Miss C. I. Kirk 6—3, 6—2; Miss W. L. Allsopp beat Miss . Minchin 6—2, 6—4; Mrs. N. Taylor beat Miss Coultman 6—3, 6—4.

LATE BIRMINGHAM SPEEDWAY RALLY

An inspired effort by Roy Dook in the last heat helped Birmingham to retain their unbeaten record in the Northern Speedway League championship at Perry Barr, Birmingham, last night, when they beat Norwich by 43 points to 41.

Unbeaten throughout with 12 points was Bert Spencer.

Cricket Wash-Out

For the second successive week and the third time in a month Birmingham League cricket was yesterday washed out by the rain. Not a ball was bowled in any of the matches.

6.6.46

Harborne Ladies' Netball Team, 1946.

The Co-operative Insurance Society Ltd. C.C., Barrows Lane, Yardley, 1950.

Ready to begin their keep-fit demonstration,
members of the 11th Birmingham Girls' Life Brigade, c. 1947.

Jack Holden Will Be Welcomed

BY TEN MILE TITLE COMPETITORS

Whether Jack Holden turns out or not, the Empire champion is assured of a great welcome at the Midland Counties 10 miles cross-country championship at Wilderness Lane, Great Barr, to-morrow.

Holden, already winner of the event on no fewer than eight occasions, was a member of the Tipton Harriers team which ended a run of 23 successive wins by Birchfield Harriers last year.

The Birchfield club will approach to-morrow's race fairly confident that they will add to their magnificent record of 46 wins out of 54 races, and the more serious opposition will come from Small Heath Harriers rather than from the reigning champions. Other clubs taking part in the event are Dudley H. and A.C., B.T.H. Rugby R.C., Coventry Godiva Harriers, Notts A.C., Smethwick Harriers, Derby and County A.C. Wolverhampton Harriers, and Sparkhill Harriers. A further nine clubs have nominated their leading men as individual entrants.

Jack Carrick, the Small Heath international, defends the individual title, and he should give his club a great start in what will probably be his last race for them in the Midlands before emigrating to Australia next month.

The Manor Abbey Sports Ground at Halesowen will be put to a new use to-morrow when it serves as headquarters for the Road Walking Association (Midland Area) 10 miles championship. The start (at 3 p.m.) and finish will be at the ground.

The Leicester Walking Club will defend the team championship against Birmingham Walking Club "A" and "B" teams, Coventry Godiva Harriers "A" and "B" teams, Lozells Harriers, R.A.R. Bridgnorth, Royal Sutton Coldfield Walking Club, and Worcester Harriers.

Last year's winner, A. Staines, Leicester W.C.), will again be on view, as will the Olympic representative, T. Lloyd Johnson. 24.2.50

7.2.52

Birmingham Rail Men in "Quiz" Contest

Saltley (Birmingham) depot of British Railways is among the 20 locomotive depots in the London Midland Region which will take part in a "quiz" competition on locomotive topics. Engine drivers, firemen and engine cleaners from each depot have formed a team of six of its members, and the winning team will go forward to an inter-regional competition. The prize for each member of the winning team will be a free sightseeing trip to France this summer, with visits to French Railways locomotive depots.

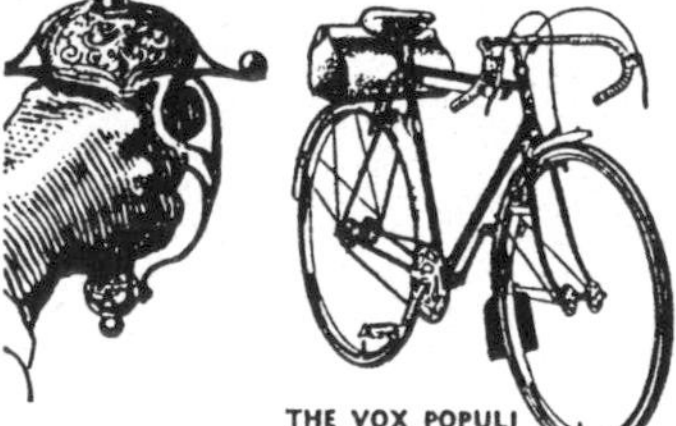

. . . TO REMIND YOU . 9/6/46

Happy Returns of the day to—

ERIC HOLLIES, Warwickshire leg-break bowler, who was born 5 June, 1912, and to

FRANK BROOME, Villa's outside-right, who first saw the light on 11 June, 1915.

And there are two veterans who must not be forgotten. They are

"TED" VIZARD, manager of "Wolves," born 7 June, 1889, and

SYDNEY SANTALL, for many years a pillar of Warwickshire who was born on 10 June, 1873.

Six years ago last Wednesday WALTER W. HART, a pioneer of Birmingham F.C., and president of the Birmingham County F.A., passed away, and it is 46 years ago to-morrow that "DADDY" MITTON, an active figure in Birmingham football circles breathed his last.

R. IVOR ("Rusty") SCORER, who has described himself as "a Yorkshireman, with red hair, thin legs and a tongue in his head," is proud of the unique honour which has come his way. He has been elected President of the Birmingham and District League while still an active playing member.

His love of cricket is well known. His war-time festivals at Edgbaston, which kept first-class cricket alive in these parts for four years, were a tribute to his organising genius.

"Rusty" played cricket for Handsworth Wood in the Birmingham League before the 1914-18 war. He has played for Moseley since 1920 and has captained the side for the last 17 years. He was in the three championship sides in 1920, 1923 and 1938. During 1921 and 1922 he assisted Warwickshire, and has played for the M.C.C., the X.L. Club, and Warwickshire Imps.

Rugby is another of his sporting interests. He has been match secretary of the North Midlands R.U. for the past 20 years. This year he was appointed to the English Rugby Union Committee. As a referee he has controlled hundreds of first-class club games and has had charge of an international trial.

His other activities include the chairmanship of the Birmingham Society for Allied Sporting Friendship. He led the sporting delegation to The Hague in 1946, and this year received a similar party from the Dutch city in Birmingham. As chairman of the Queensberry Club he has helped to organise hospitality to more than 600,000 Service men and women of the Allied Nations. 21.11.47

Kynoch's Sports' Day, Holford Drive, Perry Barr, July 1950.

Lloyds Bank Mixed Cricket Eleven, (New Street Branch),
Windermere Road Playing Fields, Moseley, c. 1952.

Viceroy C.C. Dinner, c. 1952.
Although the club was named after Viceroy Close, Edgbaston,
their home ground was in Cooksey Lane, Kingstanding.

Windspool C.C., Sheldon, c. 1952.
The team created a parks' record by bowling out Newey & Taylor C.C. for just one run!

Mike Farrell, representing Birchfield Harriers, winning the BSA 880 Yards Gold Cup, Small Heath, 7th July 1956. The same year he represented Great Britain, in the Olympic Games, at Melbourne.

Warwickshire C.C.C. Playing Staff, 1956.

Aston Villa F.C., F.A. Cup Winners, 1956/7.

Ice Skating Rink, Summer Hill Road, 14th August 1957.

Maurice Tedd hitting out for The Valor Co. Ltd. Baseball Team, Wood Lane, Erdington, 1957.

T.T. (Auto-cycle Union Tourist Trophy) replicas on display in the reception area, Norton Motors Ltd., c. 1960.

The Valor Co. Ltd. F.C., Wood Lane, Erdington, 1959.

Members of the Aston Villa and Aston and District darts' teams meet at the Boar's Head, Perry Barr, in aid of the Birmingham Mail Christmas Tree Fund, 27th May 1961.

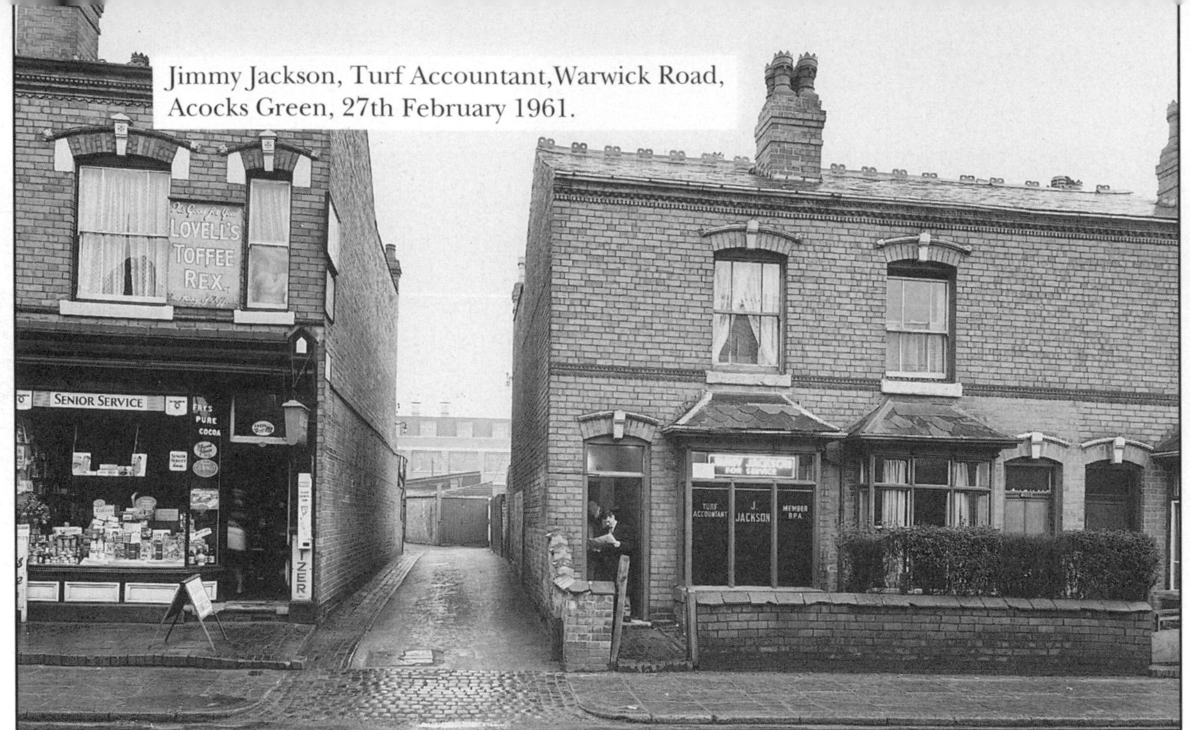

Jimmy Jackson, Turf Accountant, Warwick Road, Acocks Green, 27th February 1961.

Inter-departmental champions, R Seven Cricket Eleven, Joseph Lucas Ltd., Great King Street, Hockley, 1962.

Kynoch Rugby F.C. First Eleven, Holford Drive, Perry Barr, 1964. The club celebrated its 70th anniversary in October 1994.

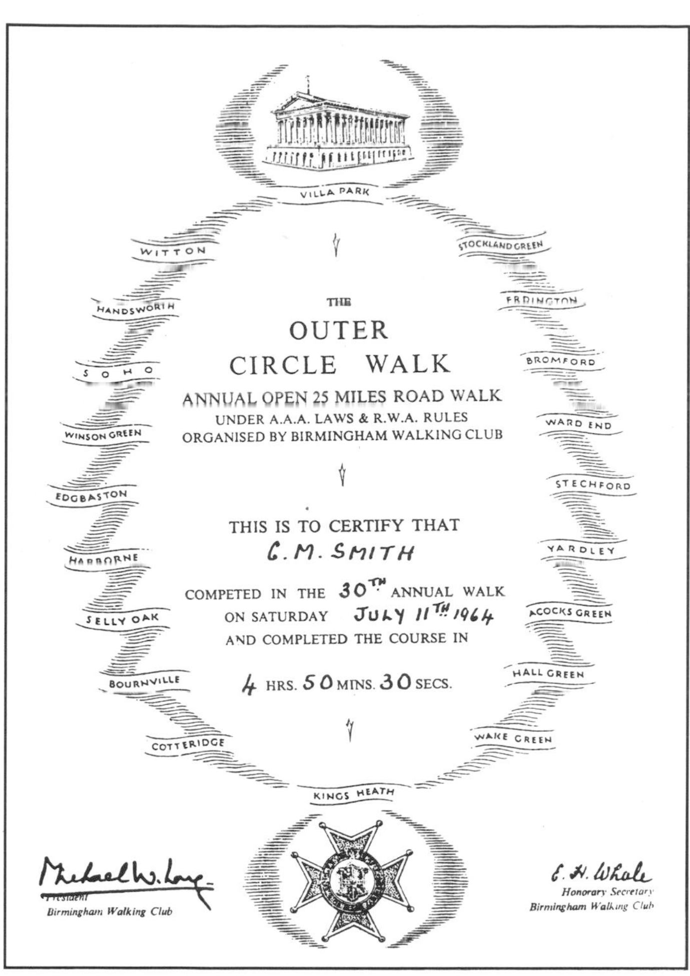

VILLA PARK
WITTON
STOCKLAND GREEN
HANDSWORTH
ERDINGTON
SOHO
BROMFORD
WINSON GREEN
WARD END
EDGBASTON
STECHFORD
HARBORNE
YARDLEY
SELLY OAK
ACOCKS GREEN
BOURNVILLE
HALL GREEN
COTTERIDGE
WAKE GREEN
KINGS HEATH

THE
OUTER
CIRCLE WALK
ANNUAL OPEN 25 MILES ROAD WALK
UNDER A.A.A. LAWS & R.W.A. RULES
ORGANISED BY BIRMINGHAM WALKING CLUB

THIS IS TO CERTIFY THAT
C. M. SMITH
COMPETED IN THE 30TH ANNUAL WALK
ON SATURDAY JULY 11TH 1964
AND COMPLETED THE COURSE IN
4 HRS. 50 MINS. 30 SECS.

Michael W. Long
President
Birmingham Walking Club

C. H. Whale
Honorary Secretary
Birmingham Walking Club

Al Cooke about to give tuition to his daughters and their friends, Silver Blades Ice Rink, Pershore Street, 1965.

The Warwick Bowl, Westley Road, Acocks Green, 8th October 1965.

"I say, old chap, they're building a new circuit."
"Who are?" "The Council."
"Where?" "In the City Centre!"
"Where," "The City Centre, NEW STREET, CORPORATION STREET, BULL STREET, COLMORE ROW."
"Good Lord, old chap, that's far seeing! What's it for?"

1970

"BRRRUM BRUM old chap"

"BRRRUM BRUM?" "Yes, the

BIRMINGHAM MOTORING FESTIVAL!

The Lord Mayor's going to open the Circuit on SEPTEMBER 1st and we'll be seeing ASTONS, FERRARIS, MASERATIS, LAMBORGHINIS, JAGS, LOTUS, CHEVRONS. I'm off now to polish my Standard 8. After all, the city is going on show, we must look our best.

"BRRRUM BRUM old chap!"
"BRRRUM BRUM!"

Bournville Social Centre

Secretary: Mr. CASSIDY

Open Daily except Sundays

BILLIARDS AND SNOOKER
FOUR FULL-SIZE TABLES
LIGHT REFRESHMENTS AVAILABLE
All at Reasonable Charges
MEMBERSHIP 10/- PER ANNUM
New Members Welcomed

DAME ELIZABETH HALL

OAK TREE LANE - BOURNVILLE, 30

Full particulars from any member of the Village Council

1969

BIRMINGHAM'S Ann Jones was the newly-crowned Queen of Wimbledon after beating the reigning champion, Billie-Jean King, 3-6, 6-3, 6-2 to win the Ladies' Singles Championship.

After a career spanning 14 years, Mrs. Jones reached the top in her 13th Wimbledon. She received the Gold Plate from Princess Anne and with it went prize money of £1,500.

There were goals galore in The South Birmingham Sunday League this week. Hall Green Saracens led the scoring spree with a mammoth 14-2 victory over Lea Bank in Division 9. Sharmans Cross cantered through to the fourth round of The President's A.M. Cup, defeating B.C.S. Utd. 10-2 while Digby Utd. surprisingly slammed Bartley Green 8-1, in their third round A.M. Challenge Shield encounter. 20.12.74

Saltley League dominoes

8.3.75

CENTRAL SECTION

	P.	W.	L.	F.	A.	P.
Pelham GO	23	16	7	191	154	32
Country Girl S	23	14	9	188	157	28
Ansells Arms	23	14	9	184	161	28
Eagle and Ball	23	14	9	171	174	28
Olive Planters	23	13	10	184	161	26
Brookhill A	23	13	10	173	172	26
Ansells B	23	12	11	181	164	24
St. Wilfreds	22	12	10	160	170	24
Packhorse	22	11	11	167	163	22
Country Girl	23	11	12	174	171	22
Brookhill C	23	10	13	173	172	20
Rock	22	10	12	165	165	20
Raven	23	10	13	169	176	20
Barley Mow	23	10	13	166	179	20
Rosary	23	10	13	164	181	20
Ward End GO	21	9	12	163	152	18
Gate	23	9	14	154	191	18
H.P.	20	5	15	125	175	10

Around 1,000 competitors and a similar number of officials are likely to attend the first sporting event booked at the National Exhibition Centre. This is for the 1977 World Table Tennis Championships — the largest championship event of its kind ever held, with competitors coming from 100 countries.

Jasper Carrott sets out to prepare the pitch, watched by some of the Birmingham City F.C. players, St Andrews, September 1977.

Handsworth Wood Boys' Schools' Under-16 hockey side, the Midlands' trophy holders, 9th March 1978.

The British Darts Cup finals, Top Rank Suite, Dale End, 30th June 1978.

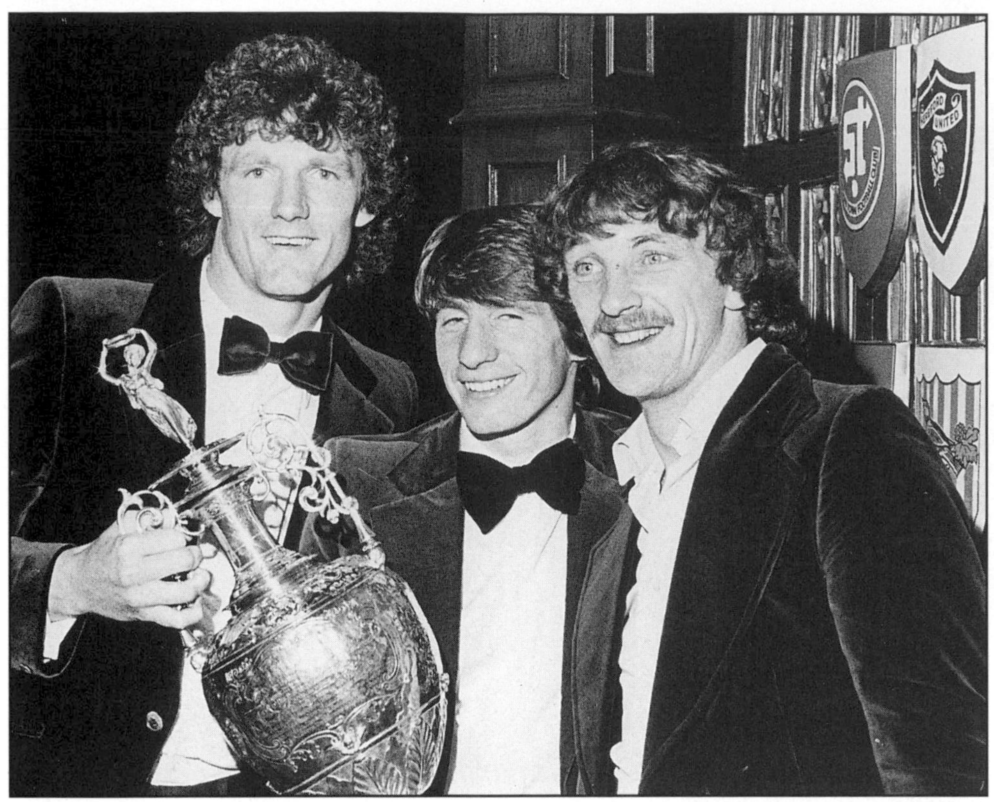

Alan Evans, Gordon Cowans and Des Bremner, of Aston Villa F.C., hold the League Championship Trophy, 1980/1.

Ready for the off. The Great Midlands' Bike Ride, Calthorpe Park, Edgbaston, 27th June 1983.

Swimming and lifesaving are just a couple of the interests for members of the Fircones (Friends in Retirement Group), Sparkhill Baths, November 1983.

Councillor Bill Turner cuts the tape to open the improved Pype Hayes Golf Course, 19th June 1984.

Braving the elements in the first Super Prix, 25th April 1986.

Olympic sprinting star, Kathy Cook (second left), joins in the celebrations shortly after presenting certificates to competitors in the qualifying hockey heats, Wyndley Leisure Centre, Sutton Coldfield, 25th February 1985. It was part of the Lord Mayor's Youth Games.

The Crown Manhattans set out for the National Pool Championships, in Blackpool, 4th November 1986. The team is based at the Crown pub, Broad Street.

Moseley Rugby F.C. players out-reach and out-number Nottingham, their opponents, 4th April 1988.

The Sunday Mercury Indoor Cricket team, 6th February 1988.

Rehearsing for the Birmingham Horse Parade, Cannon Hill Park, 21st April 1988.

The Archbishop of Birmingham, the Most Rev. Maurice Couve de Murville, takes the water at Archbishop Grimshaw School, Chelmsley Wood, July 1988. The previous day he had visited the school to say a mass and bless the new extension to the divinity centre.

Sir Garfield Sobers, former West Indies' cricket captain, at a signing session to launch his autobiography, Hudson's Bookshop, New Street, 1988. His 1958 world record Test score, of 375, was finally overtaken by Warwickshire's new signing, Brian Lara, in 1994.

Merry Christmas and a Happy New Year

Sutton Coldfield Town F.C., taking part in the BCFA Senior Cup second round, Villa Park, 21st November 1988.

The Blues bring the Leyland DAF trophy home, after beating Tranmere Rovers 3-2 at Wembley. Colmore Row, 27th May 1991.

PAT COWDELL PROMOTIONS

Matchmaker: JOHN GAYNOR

PROUDLY PRESENT

PROFESSIONAL BOXING

TOWER BALLROOM

EDGBASTON - BIRMINGHAM

DOORS OPEN 7.00 p.m | TUESDAY, 18th MAY 1993 | COMMENCE 8.00 p.m.

DOUBLE FEATURE !

MALCOLM MELVIN
(KINGS HEATH) All Ireland & Midland Area Light-Middleweight Champion

SHAUN COGAN
(SMALL HEATH) Remember his great fight with Melvin

★★★★ ★★ FULL SUPPORTING PROGRAMME FEATURING ★★ ★★ ★★

★ SPENCER McCRACKEN ★
(KINGS HEATH) Undefeated

JUSTIN CLEMENTS ★ ★ ★ PAUL HANLAN
(BIRMINGHAM) Undefeated — (BIRMINGHAM)

JAMES CAMPBELL ★ STEVE LEVENE
(BIRMINGHAM) — (BIRMINGHAM)

TICKETS: £20 Ringside : £15 : £10 Limited Number

Tickets available from Pat Cowdell 552 8082; Lynch Bros., 789 7979; Fourways Pub 559 1982; Shaun Cogan 0831 247284; Ken Rushton 559 9117; The Cauliflower Ear Pub 643 1140; Howard Clark 0860 562554; The Dubliner Pub, Digbeth 622 4729; Ernie Locke 0384 74906; Steve Levene 622 1766; Paul Chance, The Green Man Pub 0384 400532; The Witton Arms 344 4514; The Dog Pub 747 2413; The Aston Tavern 320 0456; Roundhouse Pub 770 7478; The Mountford Pub 779 4703

Pat Cowdell Promotions 129A Moat Road, Oldbury, Warley, West Midlands

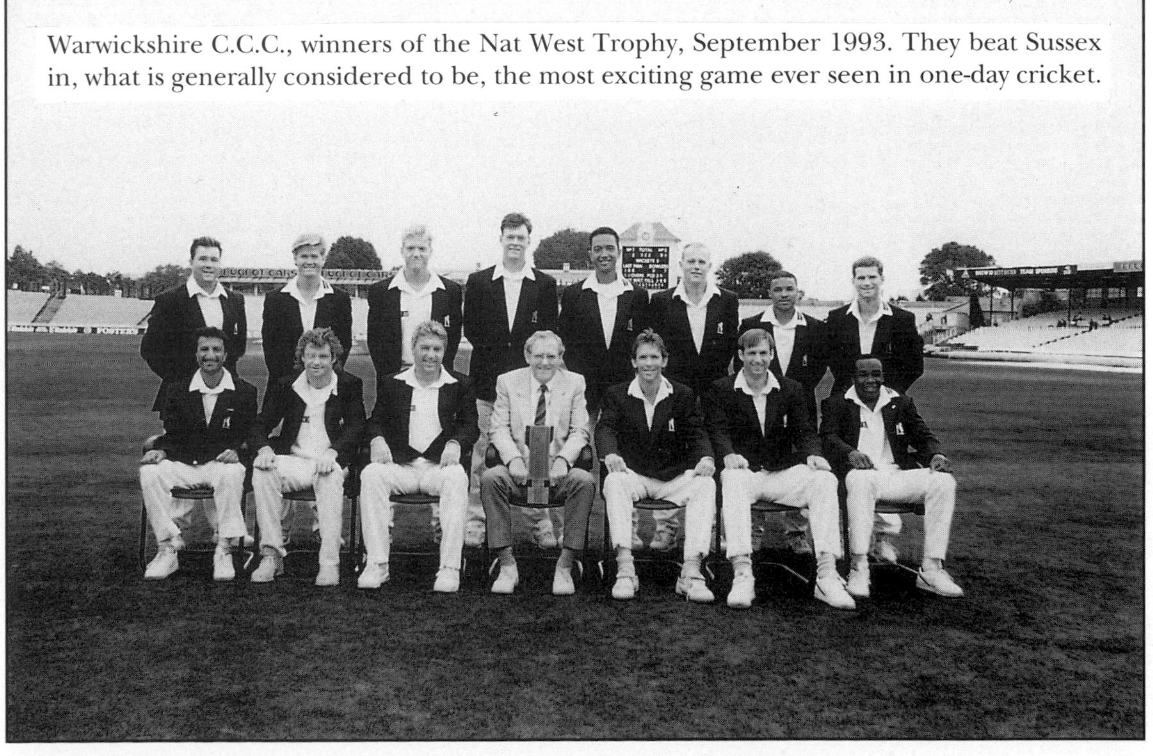

Warwickshire C.C.C., winners of the Nat West Trophy, September 1993. They beat Sussex in, what is generally considered to be, the most exciting game ever seen in one-day cricket.

LET ME ENTERTAIN YOU

BIRMINGHAM NOTES.

The Entertainment given by Anthony Diamond and Jabez White a big Success.

1897

[BY OUR RESIDENT CORRESPONDENT.]

Larry Burns and his genial friend and adviser, Pat Moran, have left Birmingham, in which city they have made a whole host of friends. Each will carry with him any amount of good wishes, and, should they return, they can rest assured of a hearty welcome.

* * *

Mr. Fred Jones, who presides over the Clements' Vaults, Newtown Row, Birmingham, is a valuable addition to the list of vocalists on the programme of smoking concerts. I hear that his services have been received by the choir-master of a church in the neighbourhood.

* * *

Anthony Diamond has secured the services of Jabez White, Charley Simpson, and Harry Tongue as assistants. His boxing academy at the rear of the "Green Lamp," Dale End, Birmingham, is being largely supported, and some likely lads will shortly emerge from Anthony's stable.

* * *

The members of the Olympic Club are disappointed that there is no likelihood of a second match between Harry Greenfield and Larry Burns taking place in Birmingham. The young American has gained a host of friends during his stay in Birmingham, and he would have no difficulty in securing a substantial backing for a second trial against the Camden Town man. Charley Tilley is also red-hot on the trail of the latter, who, however, appears to be content to rest for a while on the laurels he recently won by beating Burns.

* * *

The desire to accord Mr. Jack Brown, of Birmingham, a testimonial, is almost unanimous in the Midlands. Mr. Brown is one of the oldest supporters of the prize ring, and could be found in the corners of most of the fighters from Brum, when "things was things," to quote the expression of this great old sport. I have been deputed to look up a suitable place for the "ben" and was lucky enough to run across Mr. Harry Lyons, the genial manager of the Queen's Theatre, at the Olympic Club the other night who expressed his willingness to assist the movement in any way. A list of donations in aid of the movement has been opened; I shall be pleased to receive and acknowledge amounts, large or small, and cannot too strongly urge the claims of "one of the best" to the notice of those who admire one of the bull-dog breed who has fallen upon rough times.

* * *

Anthony Diamond and Jabez White scored a decided success last Tuesday, at the Alexandra Hall, Hope Street, Birmingham. Boxers were so plentiful that the promoters could not find room for them in the dressing-room, and it was a difficult matter to pick out the best for the show. The room was packed with a company comprising some of the best supporters of boxing in the Midlands. Mr. Harry S. Cleveland, representing the POLICE GAZETTE, was master of ceremonies and refereed the contests, and Mr. Harry Knight, late of the Birmingham Amateur Boxing Club, held the watch. Harry Adams and Harry Lee, a couple of smart amateurs, fought a five-round draw, and the rest of the programme consisted of exhibition sparring. Charley Gifford proved in his spar with Francis Mole that he has the making of a really good lad at about 8 st. 10 lbs. The brothers Parrish gave only a moderate show. Ted Phillips and Jem Gough, on the other hand, satisfied the critics to the full. Their work was clear and hard and the verdict, "good lads both," met with general approval. Fred Warner and "Darkey" Edwards were cautious but clever; on the other hand Charley Simpson and Bill Bull were clever and lively. Anthony Diamond, who retains much of the science for which he was famous about a decade ago, made matters fairly interesting for Paddy Ryan, who some years back gained prominence as "Greenfield's Dummy." Harry Tongue, a much improved Birmingham boxer, took on an old opponent in C. Barratt, a youth from Cottonopolis. The ring was hardly large enough to give them a fair chance of showing their abilities, but enabled them to "make the fur fly" during the time they were in it. Jabez White and Harvey Checketts also "fought their battles o'er again." Their set-to was a really splendid exhibition of the business. Fred Reeves, in addition to being a smart boxer, is a clever second, and shared the duties of adviser with Tom Dunn.

Alexandra Theatre,

JOHN BRIGHT STREET AND STATION STREET, BIRMINGHAM.

Proprietor and Manager .. — — — — — — — MR. LESTER COLLINGWOOD

TUESDAY, DECEMBER 12th, 1905, GRAND SPECIAL NIGHT!

THIRD ANNIVERSARY OF MR.

LESTER COLLINGWOOD

At 7-15 Prompt the Curtain will Rise on Mr.

J. A. CAMPBELL'S

NEW HOMELY DRAMA, ENTITLED,

THE LITTLE BREADWINNER

IN FOUR ACTS.

Lord William Dorrington, a Quaker.......... Mr. J. A. CAMPBELL
Richard Lawrence, his adopted Son.......... Mr. EVAN ROBERTS
Joseph Prior, confidential Secretary to Lord William...... Mr. ROLAND YORKE
Charles Prior, Brother to Joseph.......... Mr. ALLEN CHARLES
Doctor Chadwick, of the Lambeth Hospital .. Mr. WALLE SPINNER
Monty, a Pugilist.......... Mr. LEA HAIR
Servant, at Dorrington Hall.......... Mr. THOMAS MINNS
Detective.......... Mr. HENRY LOWTHER
Margaret Daventry, Granddaughter of Lord William.......... Miss MARY MALLALIEU
Bridget O'Flanagan, Housekeeper at Dorrington.......... Miss JENNY BOSTOCK
Kate Cherry, in Love with Joseph Prior .. Miss MAUD BUCHANAN
Ruth Cherry, Sister to Kate.......... Miss EMMIE LITCHFIELD
AND
Meg, "The Little Breadwinner"...... LITTLE EMMIE THOMAS

— MUSIC. —

OVERTURE .. "The Little Breadwinner" .. *Arthur Workman*
SELECTION .. .. "Mikado" .. .. *Arthur Sullivan*
WALTZ .. .. "Venetienne" .. .. *Waldteufel*
VALSE LENTE .. "Amoureuse" .. .. .. *Berger*

Conductor - - - - Mr. A. W. PARRY.

To be followed immediately by the following Variety Artistes—

1.—MISS EDIE RIVERS,
The Charming Fairy of the Alexandra Aladdin Pantomime.
2.—BURLEY BROTHERS (Gaiety).
3.—PROFESSOR ALBERTO (Local).
The well-known Prestidigitateur and Illusionist.
4.—FRED CECIL & HAROLD HASTINGS
In their Summer Idiosyncracies.
5.—The BIRMINGHAM BANJO QUARTETTE (Local)
6.—MISS ROSE ELLIOTT (Gaiety).
7.—DEL LEVY, Burlesque Artiste.
8.—MR. FRANK SEELEY (Gaiety).
9.—ZANFRETTO AND NAPIO (Gaiety).
10.—SLADE MURRAY (Gaiety).
11.—THOS. E. FINGLASS (Hippodrome).
12.—JOCK WHITEFORD (Hippodrome).
13.—SYD SYLVESTER (Local),
Patter Comedian.
14.—J. H. CRUISE (Local).
Will sing "Statues in Victoria Square."
15.—JORDAN & HARVEY (Empire),
Hebrew Dialect Performers.

By kind permission of Albert Bushell, Esq., Thomas Barrasford, Esq., P. D. Elbourne, Esq., Oswald Stoll, Esq., A. W. Matcham, Esq.

AUGMENTED ORCHESTRA, Under the Conductorship of Mr. ARTHUR PARRY.
Stage Manager, Mr. HARRY CALVER.

BOXING NIGHT, DECEMBER 26th,

At 7-30, will be produced LESTER COLLINGWOOD'S Third Birmingham Pantomime,

"BLUE BEARD."

Assistant Acting Manager} For Mr. LESTER COLLINGWOOD {.......Mr. FRED BERNARDO
Secretary.......... Miss L. JEPHCOTT
Bill Inspector.......... Mr. JOHN CLAMP
Master Carpenter.......... Mr. W. S. JONES
Property Master.......... Mr. A. HARRISON

IN ACCORDANCE WITH THE REQUIREMENTS OF THE BIRMINGHAM LICENSING JUSTICES:—

The Public may leave at the end of the performance by all exits and entrance doors, and such doors must at that time be open.

All Gangways, Passages, and Staircases must be kept entirely free from chairs or any other obstructions.

The Safety Curtain must be lowered about the middle of the performance, so as to ensure its being in proper working order.

James Upton, Printer, Birmingham.

Digbeth Institute Brass Band, 1912.

Telephone Midland 541.

MONDAY, OCT. 4th, 1920 TWICE NIGHTLY at 6-30 & 8-35

GEORGE
MOZART
IN NEW TYPES

PERCY
HONRI
AND HIS CONCERTINA.

LONDON'S FAVOURITE ENTERTAINERS
KING & BENSON
Present their New Offering, "TRULY RURAL." By R. P. Weston & Bert Lee.

LATEST NEWS PICTURES.

JACK MERRITT
THE ROUNDING MARVEL

DE WYNNE BROS.
PRESENTING THEIR CLASSICAL ATHLETIC ACT

ANSEROUL TROUPE
KINGS OF DOUBLE AND TREBLE SOMERSAULTS

Erdington Cottage Homes' Brass Band, c. 1913.

The Grand Picture Palace, Soho Road, Handsworth, c. 1924.

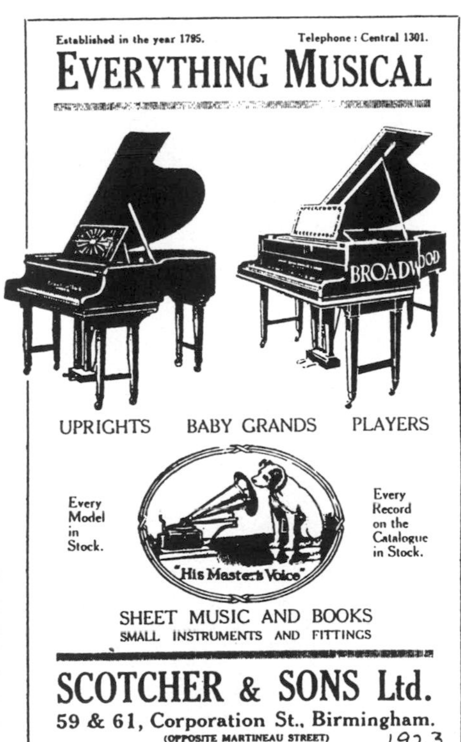

15.7.26

Read the remarkable interview with

SIR ARTHUR CONAN DOYLE

(Creator of "Sherlock Holmes")

Exclusive in this week's

Sunday Mercury

Millions have read his books but few enjoy his confidences. A writer of keen discernment and established reputation, Sir Arthur also gives his views on some of the vital questions of the day.

Order your Sunday Mercury

THE "ELITE" THEATRE

BORDESLEY GREEN, BIRMINGHAM

Full Variety Programme—Twice Nightly—6-45 & 8-45

One of the Finest Orchestras in Greater Birmingham. Beautifully equipped.
If you have not visited this Theatre, why not?

BOOK YOUR SEATS—"VICTORIA 169" 1922

PHYLLIS BRADLEY
SOPRANO
MIDLAND OPERA SOCIETY
TOWN HALL AND
PROVINCIAL CONCERTS

"SERPOLETTE"
IN
"Les Cloches de Corneville"

FOR ENGAGEMENTS:
BEETHOVEN VILLA
POPLAR ROAD
EDGBASTON, BIRMINGHAM
OR TELEPHONE No. C7392

1923

MUSIC

is infinitely more enjoyable when played by the best instrumentalists. In fact, the quality of the musician is as great a factor as the quality of the music to be played when it comes to enjoyment. Both are perfection at

THE
Grange Super Cinema
Coventry Road, Small Heath

Theatre Royal, Birmingham.
Commencing MONDAY, OCT. 5th, 1925
For Six Evenings at 7-15.
Matinees, Thursday and Saturday at 2 p.m.

Personal Visit of . . .
SIR
Frank Benson
and his Company in Plays of
SHAKESPEARE
and OLD ENGLISH COMEDIES.

REPERTOIRE:
MONDAY EVENING: THE MERCHANT OF VENICE
TUESDAY EVENING:—SHERIDAN'S COMEDY THE RIVALS
WEDNESDAY EVENING: THE TEMPEST
THURSDAY MATINEE: JULIUS CÆSAR
THURSDAY EVENING: HAMLET
FRIDAY EVENING -GOLDSMITH'S COMEDY SHE STOOPS TO CONQUER
SATURDAY MATINEE: THE MERCHANT OF VENICE
SATURDAY EVENING—SHERIDAN'S COMEDY THE SCHOOL FOR SCANDAL

MATTERS MUSICAL

Being the Second of a Series of Letters from our Musical Director to the Patrons of Lozells Picture House.

Ladies and Gentlemen,

As a result of your keen interest and co-operation, our Friday evening "REQUEST NIGHT PROGRAMMES" have proven quite a success, and they will therefore continue to be a feature of the entertainment at L.P.H.

I trust that all who sent requests to me during October were perfectly satisfied with our performance of their favoured work. Since our first "Request Night" I have received quite a number of letters expressing appreciation of our efforts. I assure you that such acknowledgment is both encouraging and sincerely appreciated by my orchestra and myself.

During the second week of October I received so many requests for our Friday evening programme that it was quite impossible to play every number requested, for the playing would have taken at least six hours. I was therefore forced to solve the problem as to which numbers we should play, by selecting those which had been asked for by the majority. As this plan may have caused a little disappointment to one or two, I think a better plan for the future will be for us to play request items *in the order in which I receive them.* Therefore to avoid disappointment will you please let me know your wishes as early as possible each week?

Within the last month I have also received many letters asking questions regarding the music we play. I trust that my replies have been as interesting to the recipients as their letters have been to me. The majority of the questions I have been asked have been about the "meaning" or "story" connected to different works which we have played. These questions have proven to me that there are undoubtedly very many who listen whenever we are playing and are keenly interested in the music and "what it is all about." I therefore have decided that my letter in next month's issue of this booklet will be solely upon one subject, namely—"Listening to, *and understanding,* Music." For the moment I will simply say that music may be as vulgar as the lowest type of comedy, or as stupid as the worst treatises of the most pedantic grammarian. It may rise into such heights of beauty and grandeur as no other art can reach; it may carry us to the edge of eternity, where we may hear unutterable things. The choice between these is always in our own minds, but if we come to music eager to learn its mysteries and beauty, we will be rewarded with a happiness beyond all pleasures and will live with us forever.

Yours faithfully,

ERNEST A. PARSONS,
Musical Director.

1928

If winter is anything like summer you will need the MARCONIPHONE on many gray days—but there's no need to make them grayer by waiting to purchase outright. The latest Marconiphone can be in your home, passing gayly for you the hours of the very next "gray day" for the sum of 20/- down. The Model 22 is easy to operate, the Marconiphone "Popular" Loud-Speaker gives utmost volume and clarity, while the cabinet itself is a decorative piece of furniture. It is the best—but you can afford it. The balance of twelve monthly payments of 18/1 are paid off while you enjoy your own set.

BRANDES
RADIO PRODUCTS
QUALITY
AT A
MODERATE PRICE

BRANDESET IIIA.
£7 5s. 0d.
including
Valves and Royalty.
The Set with the Marvellous Range, combined with purity of Tone. Simplicity with Results.

THE ELLIPTICON.
£3 17s. 6d.
Results as near Perfection as possible, and unequalled at double the price. A handsome fitment in Mahogany, Oak or Walnut.

THE BRANDOLA.
£2 10s. 0d.
For those who prefer the horn type loud speaker. Designed to use minimum current output and to give exceptional clarity over the full range. Neutral brown finish.

TERMS: £1 DEPOSIT SECURES THIS SET.

A. GOODMAN
BRANDES AND MARCONIPHONE SERVICE AGENT,
53, Lozells Road :: Birmingham.
(Directly opposite this Theatre). Telephone No.: Northern 252.

ACCUMULATOR CHARGING DEPÔT
SERVICE AND EFFICIENCY AT REASONABLE CHARGES.

1928

The Grand Theatre, Corporation Street, 1930.

NEW ATTRACTIONS IN BIRMINGHAM.

REPERTORY AND PRINCE OF WALES THEATRES.

1932

Changes of the Christmas season programme at two of the principal theatres in the city are to be noted next week. The pantomimes, "Robinson Crusoe," at the Alexandra Theatre, and "Mother Goose," at the Theatre Royal, are drawing excellent houses, and will run for several more weeks, but the D'Oyly Carte Opera Co. conclude their season at the Prince of Wales Theatre to-night, and "The Barretts of Wimpole Street" has been taken off at the Repertory Theatre. At the former theatre light opera will again be the fare. "Tantivy Towers," the new English comic opera, which is the combined work of A. P. Herbert and Thomas F. Dunhill, as author and composer, will be staged, and as it has been compared favourably with the work of Gilbert and Sullivan, local theatre goers will have a ready opportunity to test the worth of this view. It was produced in London by Sir Nigel Playfair and the story deals with the clash which occurs between artistic "Chelsea" and the "county" devoted to "huntin', fishin' and shootin'." The cast includes Trefor Jones, Doris Woodall, Kathleen Lafla, George Bishop and Leonard S. Daniels.

"Street Scene," Elmer Rice's notable drama, which had a successful run in London last year, will be produced by Mr. Maxwell Wray at the Repertory Theatre, entering on a run of three weeks, with a possible extension if necessary. The scene, as many will be aware, is set outside a New York tenement house, and there are something like seventy characters representing the varied types and nationalities to be found in New York. Arthur Prince, the ventriloquist, is striking out on a new line by running a "road show," which he calls "Here We Are." It will be seen at the Empire. Mr. Prince's sailor Boy Jim is supplemented by "Monty," a life-size walking figure in a new sketch, "A Night in New York." The artists who will share in the show include Miss José Collins, Miss Dorrie Dene, Lawrence Barclay (the author of "Our Lodger's Such a Nice Young Man") and a number of others.

The Hippodrome returns to lightning vaudeville with a nine-acts programme in which the Royal Tzigane Band will be the principal attraction. The others include Herman Hyde and Selly Burrill (an American duo), the Two New Bobs, De Biere, the magician, the Tom Davis Trio, the Dinky Denton Trio, Lilian Fitzroy, Stan Annison and Evelyn Major, and the Juggling Demons.

The Grand Theatre will give a combination of vaudeville acts, under the title "Vaudeville Menu of 1932," with the Seven De Guise Seymours (a family of musicians, all born and living in Birmingham), James Hunter (the humorist), Billy Kay (another comedian), Joe and Ida, and Darty and Partner.

The opening of the Tudor Cinema, Kings Heath, 30th March 1929.

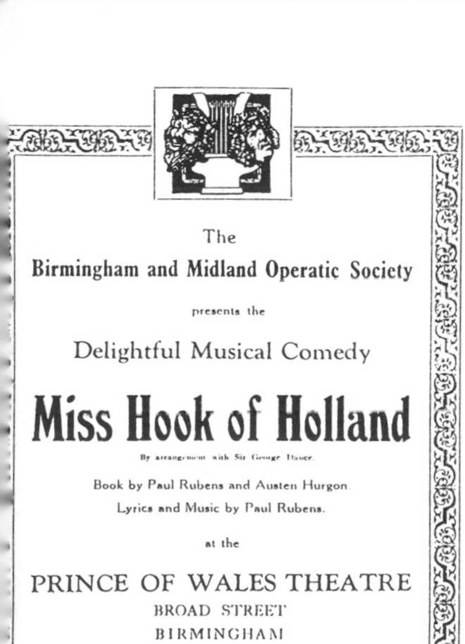
The

Birmingham and Midland Operatic Society

presents the

Delightful Musical Comedy

Miss Hook of Holland

By arrangement with Sir George Dance.

Book by Paul Rubens and Austen Hurgon.
Lyrics and Music by Paul Rubens.

at the

PRINCE OF WALES THEATRE
BROAD STREET
BIRMINGHAM

for 6 nights

NOVEMBER 30th to DECEMBER 5th, 1931

Fred Kitchen and Billy Merson in "Babes in the Wood", Alexandra Theatre, 1933/4.

Northfield Church Operatic Society in costume for their production of "San Toy", 1931. After the war the company amalgamated with the Rubery St Chad's Amateur Operatic Society and are known, to this day, as the Northfield Amateur Operatic Society.

SATURDAY NEXT, AUGUST 22ND. 1936.

THE SEVENTH ANNUAL

FLOWER SHOW, BABY SHOW & CARNIVAL

FANCY DRESS COMPETITION & PARADE

— AT —

HAWKESLEY HALL, MILL WALK.

CROWNING of the FLOWER QUEEN and JUDGING at 2.15 p.m.

GRAND PARADE TO THE SHOW GROUND, BRISTOL ROAD SOUTH.
(Corner of Tessall Lane.)

LONGBRIDGE'S DAY OUT. *COME AND BE INTERESTED AND AMUSED.*

MANY ATTRACTIONS ON THE SHOW GROUND.

FULL FUN FAIR

LADIES' ANKLE COMPETITION

Refreshments at Moderate Charges.

Public Address Equipment and Music by WALLACE & CO., COTTERIDGE.

Competitions Freak Golf Gold Fish Skittles, etc.

BABY SHOW

JUDGING COMMENCES AT 4 P.M.

EXHIBITS OF HANDICRAFT, HORTICULTURE AND GARDEN SPECIALITIES.

DISPLAY OF DANCING by Pupils of the DAURE SCHOOL OF DANCING.

PILLOW FIGHTING BY THE LICKEY ROVERS.
(By kind permission of W. A. HOWITT, Esq.)

ADMISSION TO GROUND - SIXPENCE

TICKETS PURCHASED BEFORE THE DAY OF SHOW - 4d. EACH

OPEN AT 2 P.M.

Tickets, Schedules and Entry Forms obtainable at any of the Addresses on Next Page.

SILVER JUBILEE

SOUVENIR RECORDS

with

PICTORIAL SOUVENIR LABEL IN SIX COLOURS

JACK PAYNE & HIS BAND

8455. **JUBILEE CELEBRATION SELECTION**

With Choruses

Parts 1 & 2. 'Say it with Music,' 'Coronation Day,' 'Song d'Automne,' 'Everybody's doing it,' 'Tipperary,' 'Soldiers of the King,' 'Hearts of Oak,' 'When Johnnie comes marching home again.' 'Coal Black Mammy,' 'Round the Marble Arch,' 'Love is the Sweetest thing,' 'Here's a Health unto his Majesty.'

BAND OF H.M. WELSH GUARDS

8457 **SILVER JUBILEE MEMORIES (1910-1935)**

Vocalist—Foster Richardson

Parts 1 & 2. 'Coronation Bells,' 'Indian Music,' 'Royal Salute,' 'British Grenadiers,' 'Heiland Laddie,' 'Minuet,' 'Rule Britannia,' 'God Bless the Prince of Wales,' 'Life on the Ocean Wave,' 'Pack up your troubles,' 'Here's a Health unto his Majesty,' 'God save the King.'

BAND OF H.M. WELSH GUARDS

With Foster Richardson, Children's Choir and Grand Organ.

8456 **LET US SING UNTO THEIR MAJESTIES.**
LAND OF HOPE AND GLORY. 1935

CRESCENT PLAYERS IN BRILLIANT PLAY

1936

THE Crescent Theatre players presented at the theatre, last night, Sean O'Casey's "The Plough and the Stars," a dramatic peep at the Irish rebellion of 1916.

This is a play of brilliant entries and brilliant exits; of brilliant lines and brilliant wit.

But underneath the brililance there is life. And the spirit is the spirit of Ireland, the tears and the laughter of it, the poetry of it, and the anguished cry of it, the stark realities of it, and the wild imaginings of it . . .

The action takes place mostly in a tenement flat in Dublin, where half-a-dozen characters live. The characters are typically Irish, the same characters that you find in all Irish plays and books—the young Communist, the old general, the quarreling women . . . .

But they live.

Always they are doing something. For instance, at the beginning, Fluther, the carpenter, is mending the door, Nora is getting tea for her Jackie, Mrs. Gogan is hunting in a cupboard and Uncle Peter is wrestling with a collar as stiff as steel. Partly this was the dramatist at work but partly too it was the work of producer Mayors' Secretary, Norman Leaker.

That production was effective because it was simple, unobtrusive, providing *only* a background for the grim goings-on.

In a cast of all-round excellence, three characters stood out, not as good, but as masterpieces, they were Harry Hunt, as Fluther, Joan Simpson as Mrs. Gogan, and Mabel France as Bessie Burgess. Those stood out—because they were even more lively than the rest.

I.A.

Bandleader Jack Payne.

BARRIE PLAY AT KING'S NORTON SCHOOL

XMAS 1937

CREDITABLE PRODUCTION OF "THE ADMIRABLE CRICHTON"

Sir James Barrie's "The Admirable Crichton" was presented at the King's Norton Secondary School for Boys last night by a company which included a few members of the school staff. Others in the company were the pupils at the school, and together they gave a creditable production.

The scenery was painted by the school pupils and the furnishings, with the exception of a few articles, were made in the manual room. The cast was as follows:—T. V. Sheppard, who played Crichton; C. E. Cole, C. Stockdale, M. H. Redrup, L. Ostrov, D. W. Spafford, J. H. Bishop, R. Roberts, P. R. Barratt, M. B. Wheeler, W. H. Duggins, K. Bailey, J. R. Sanders, R. H. Moores and W. Lavender. A programme of music was given by the school orchestra.

The Paramount Theatre, Birmingham, which has been erected on the former site of the King Edward's High School in New Street, is to open on Saturday evening, September 4. For some time the structure of the cinema itself—which, with its attendant offices and shops, represents a venture costing about £850,000—has been completed, but much interior work remains to be done during the next two and a half weeks.

The auditorium is still almost entirely occupied by scaffolding, and, apart from boilers for the heating system, no equipment has been installed. Engineers are about to erect up-to-date ventilation plant, which will control and cleanse every cubic inch of air passed through the auditorium; to prepare lighting facilities so elaborate that, it is claimed, grand opera could be staged without additional apparatus, and to instal an intricate system of vacuum cleaning.

The theatre will seat 2,600 people—1,600 in the stalls and 1,000 in the circle. There will be a permanent staff of nearly a hundred, of whom a proportion was chosen yesterday by Mr. Leslie C. Holderness, of the Paramount office in London, who has had charge of the inauguration of all the new Paramount theatres and will be in control until the cinema has become established. 18.8.37

The Mayfair Cinema, College Road, Kingstanding, 1939.

Pigeons being released from the roof of Broadcasting House, Broad Street, during a reconstruction of an old-time pigeon race by clock, 5th April 1939. This was part of the Children's Hour programme, conducted by Enid Maxwell and the birds flew to Chesterfield.

CONJURERS 1939

Mr. W. J. MERRIFIELD, of Monument-road, Birmingham, writes :—

This is about conjurers.

Why do they :

1. Labour under the impression that every member of the audience has just passed his fourth birthday?

2. Wear a ghastly, artificial grin, peculiar to themselves?

3. Blame the spirits when things go wrong?

4. Use inane expressions, such as: "This is an egg"?

5. Pose in an attitude reminiscent of chronic gout?

6. Everlastingly cadge watches and rings?

Was Barnum right, or are TWO suckers born every minute?

***ANSWER**: Our only conjuring trick being the removal of unused stamps from envelopes, is there a conjurer in the house who'd care to take this little load on?*

Annual Concert Party, St John Ambulance HQ, Lionel Street, 1938.

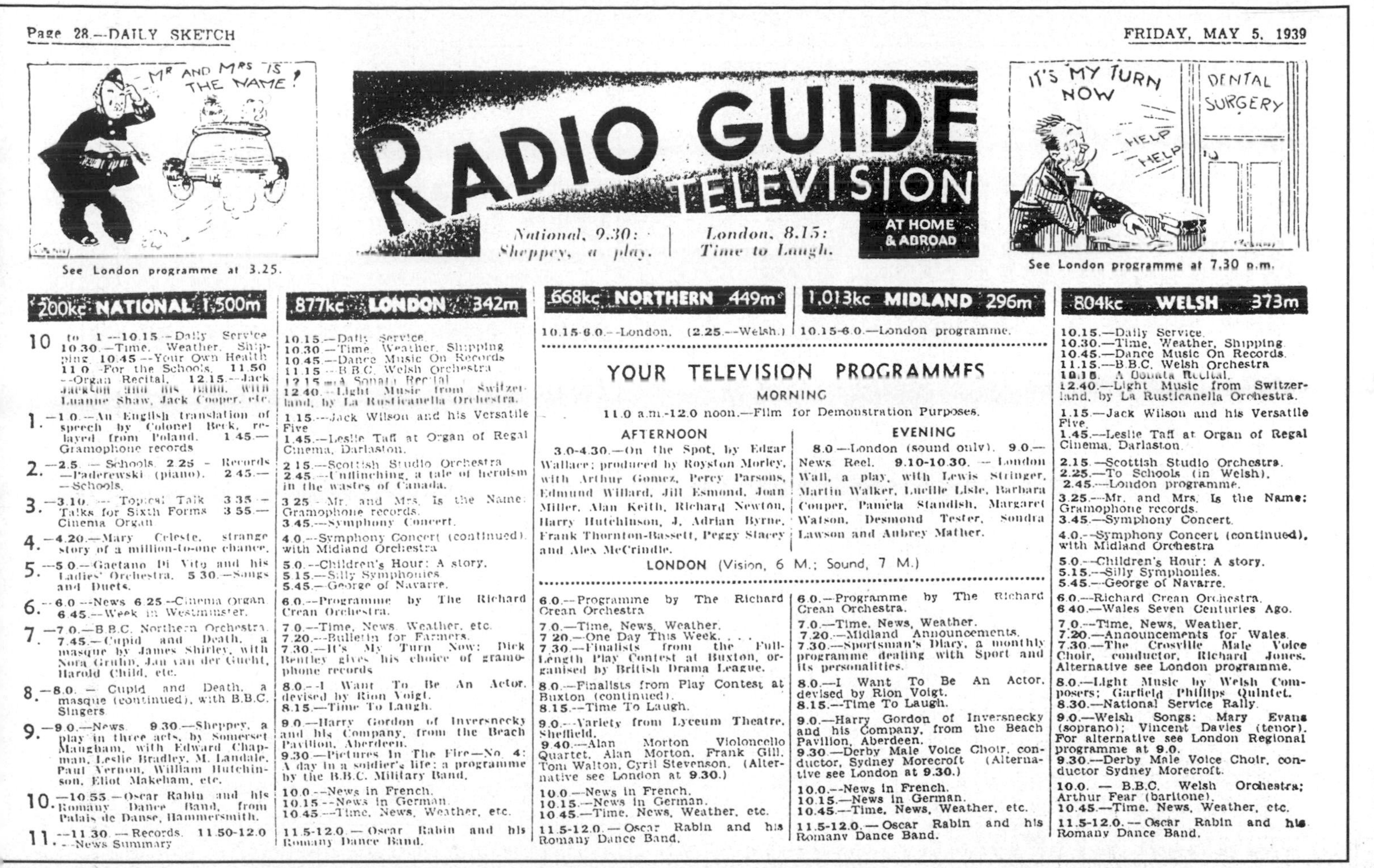

Page 28.—DAILY SKETCH FRIDAY, MAY 5, 1939

See London programme at 3.25.

National, 9.30: Sheppey, a play. | *London, 8.15: Time to Laugh.*

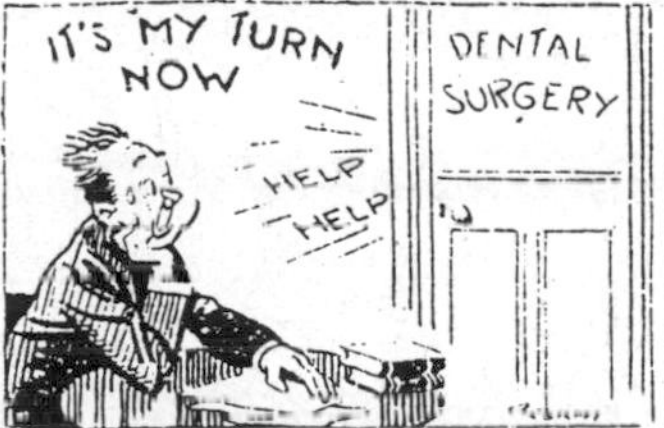

See London programme at 7.30 p.m.

200kc NATIONAL 1,500m

10 to 1.—10.15.—Daily Service. 10.30.—Time. Weather. Shipping. 10.45.—Your Own Health. 11.0.—For the Schools. 11.50.—Organ Recital. 12.15.—Jack Jackson and his Band, with Luanne Shaw, Jack Cooper, etc.

1.—1.0.—An English translation of speech by Colonel Beck, relayed from Poland. 1.45.—Gramophone records

2.—2.5. — Schools. 2.25 - Records —Paderewski (piano). 2.45.—Schools.

3.—3.10. — Topical Talk 3.35 — Talks for Sixth Forms 3.55.—Cinema Organ

4.—4.20.—Mary Celeste, strange story of a million-to-one chance.

5.—5.0.—Gaetano Di Vito and his Ladies' Orchestra. 5.30.—Songs and Duets.

6.—6.0.—News 6.25.—Cinema Organ. 6.45.—Week in Westminster.

7.—7.0.—B.B.C. Northern Orchestra. 7.45.—Cupid and Death, a masque by James Shirley, with Nora Gruhn, Jan van der Gucht, Harold Child, etc.

8.—8.0. — Cupid and Death, a masque (continued), with B.B.C. Singers

9.—9.0.—News 9.30.—Sheppey, a play in three acts, by Somerset Maugham, with Edward Chapman, Leslie Bradley, M. Landale, Paul Vernon, William Hutchinson, Eliot Makeham, etc.

10.—10.55.—Oscar Rabin and his Romany Dance Band, from Palais de Danse, Hammersmith.

11.—11.30. — Records. 11.50-12.0.—News Summary

877kc LONDON 342m

10.15.—Daily Service.
10.30.—Time. Weather. Shipping
10.45.—Dance Music On Records
11.15.—B.B.C. Welsh Orchestra
12.15.—A Sonata Recital
12.40.—Light Music from Switzerland, by La Rusticanella Orchestra.

1.15.—Jack Wilson and his Versatile Five
1.45.—Leslie Taff at Organ of Regal Cinema, Darlaston.

2.15.—Scottish Studio Orchestra
2.45.—Unflinching, a tale of heroism in the wastes of Canada.

3.25.—Mr. and Mrs. Is the Name: Gramophone records.
3.45.—Symphony Concert.

4.0.—Symphony Concert (continued), with Midland Orchestra

5.0.—Children's Hour: A story.
5.15.—Silly Symphonies
5.45.—George of Navarre.

6.0.—Programme by The Richard Crean Orchestra.

7.0.—Time, News, Weather, etc.
7.20.—Bulletin for Farmers.
7.30.—It's My Turn Now: Dick Bentley gives his choice of gramophone records

8.0.—I Want To Be An Actor, devised by Rion Voigt.
8.15.—Time To Laugh.

9.0.—Harry Gordon of Inversnecky and his Company, from the Beach Pavilion, Aberdeen.
9.30.—Pictures In The Fire—No. 4: A day in a soldier's life; a programme by the B.B.C. Military Band.

10.0.—News in French.
10.15.—News in German.
10.45.—Time, News, Weather, etc.

11.5-12.0. — Oscar Rabin and his Romany Dance Band.

668kc NORTHERN 449m

10.15-6.0.—London. (2.25.—Welsh.)

1,013kc MIDLAND 296m

10.15-6.0.—London programme.

YOUR TELEVISION PROGRAMMES

MORNING

11.0 a.m.-12.0 noon.—Film for Demonstration Purposes.

AFTERNOON

3.0-4.30.—On the Spot, by Edgar Wallace; produced by Royston Morley, with Arthur Gomez, Percy Parsons, Edmund Willard, Jill Esmond, Joan Miller, Alan Keith, Richard Newton, Harry Hutchinson, J. Adrian Byrne, Frank Thornton-Bassett, Peggy Stacey and Alex McCrindle.

EVENING

8.0.—London (sound only). 9.0.—News Reel. 9.10-10.30. — London Wall, a play, with Lewis Stringer, Martin Walker, Lucille Lisle, Barbara Couper, Pamela Standish, Margaret Watson, Desmond Tester, Sondra Lawson and Aubrey Mather.

LONDON (Vision, 6 M.; Sound, 7 M.)

NORTHERN

6.0.—Programme by The Richard Crean Orchestra

7.0.—Time, News, Weather.
7.20.—One Day This Week. . . .
7.30.—Finalists from the Full-Length Play Contest at Buxton, organised by British Drama League.

8.0.—Finalists from Play Contest at Buxton (continued).
8.15.—Time To Laugh.

9.0.—Variety from Lyceum Theatre, Sheffield.
9.40.—Alan Morton Violoncello Quartet. Alan Morton, Frank Gill, Tom Walton, Cyril Stevenson. (Alternative see London at 9.30.)

10.0.—News in French.
10.15.—News in German.
10.45.—Time, News, Weather, etc.

11.5-12.0. — Oscar Rabin and his Romany Dance Band.

MIDLAND

6.0.—Programme by The Richard Crean Orchestra.

7.0.—Time, News, Weather.
7.20.—Midland Announcements.
7.30.—Sportsman's Diary, a monthly programme dealing with Sport and its personalities.

8.0.—I Want To Be An Actor, devised by Rion Voigt.
8.15.—Time To Laugh.

9.0.—Harry Gordon of Inversnecky and his Company, from the Beach Pavilion, Aberdeen.
9.30.—Derby Male Voice Choir, conductor, Sydney Morecroft (Alternative see London at 9.30.)

10.0.—News in French.
10.15.—News in German.
10.45.—Time, News, Weather, etc.

11.5-12.0. — Oscar Rabin and his Romany Dance Band.

804kc WELSH 373m

10.15.—Daily Service.
10.30.—Time, Weather, Shipping.
10.45.—Dance Music On Records.
11.15.—B.B.C. Welsh Orchestra
12.15.—A Sonata Recital.
12.40.—Light Music from Switzerland, by La Rusticanella Orchestra.

1.15.—Jack Wilson and his Versatile Five.
1.45.—Leslie Taff at Organ of Regal Cinema, Darlaston.

2.15.—Scottish Studio Orchestra.
2.25.—To Schools (in Welsh).
2.45.—London programme.

3.25.—Mr. and Mrs. Is the Name: Gramophone records.
3.45.—Symphony Concert.

4.0.—Symphony Concert (continued), with Midland Orchestra

5.0.—Children's Hour: A story.
5.15.—Silly Symphonies.
5.45.—George of Navarre.

6.0.—Richard Crean Orchestra.
6.40.—Wales Seven Centuries Ago.

7.0.—Time, News, Weather.
7.20.—Announcements for Wales.
7.30.—The Crosville Male Voice Choir, conductor, Richard Jones. Alternative see London programme.

8.0.—Light Music by Welsh Composers; Garfield Phillips Quintet.
8.30.—National Service Rally.

9.0.—Welsh Songs: Mary Evans (soprano); Vincent Davies (tenor). For alternative see London Regional programme at 9.0.
9.30.—Derby Male Voice Choir, conductor Sydney Morecroft.

10.0. — B.B.C. Welsh Orchestra; Arthur Fear (baritone).
10.45.—Time, News, Weather, etc.

11.5-12.0. — Oscar Rabin and his Romany Dance Band.

Harry Pell rehearses the Hippodrome Orchestra, c. 1942.

Western Union (20th Century-Fox, 1941), directed by Fritz Lang

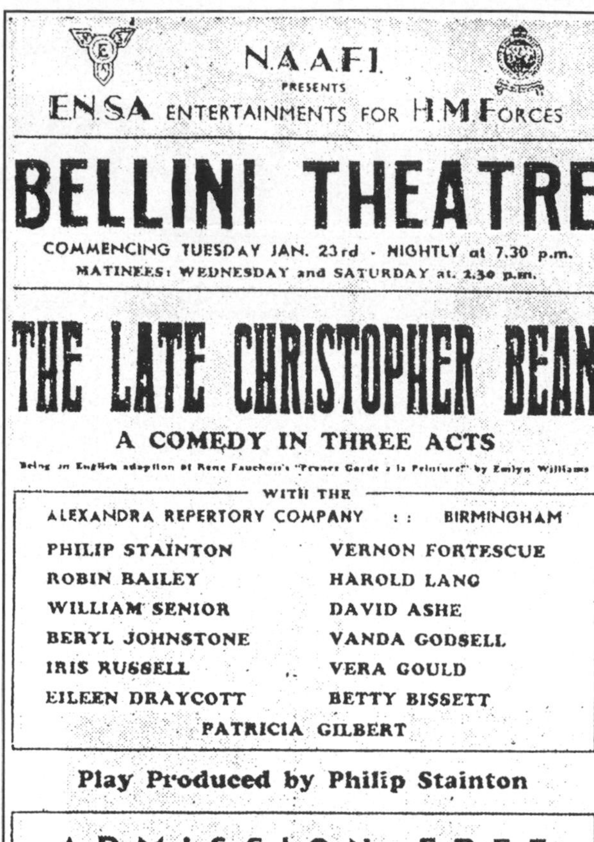
N.A.A.F.I.
PRESENTS
E.N.S.A. ENTERTAINMENTS FOR H.M. FORCES

BELLINI THEATRE

COMMENCING TUESDAY JAN. 23rd · NIGHTLY at 7.30 p.m.
MATINEES: WEDNESDAY and SATURDAY at 2.30 p.m.

THE LATE CHRISTOPHER BEAN

A COMEDY IN THREE ACTS

Being an English adaption of Rene Fauchois's "Prenez Garde a la Peinture" by Emlyn Williams

WITH THE
ALEXANDRA REPERTORY COMPANY :: BIRMINGHAM

PHILIP STAINTON — VERNON FORTESCUE
ROBIN BAILEY — HAROLD LANG
WILLIAM SENIOR — DAVID ASHE
BERYL JOHNSTONE — VANDA GODSELL
IRIS RUSSELL — VERA GOULD
EILEEN DRAYCOTT — BETTY BISSETT
PATRICIA GILBERT

Play Produced by Philip Stainton

ADMISSION FREE

The Alexandra Theatre's Repertory Company entertaining the troops, in Italy, 1945.

Sparkbrook comedian, Sid Field and Margaret Lockwood in the 1946 film "Cardboard Cavalier".

Robin Bailey, a regular with the Alexandra Repertory Company and still appearing on television to this day.

CITY AND MIDLAND ITEMS

20/4/45

PLAYS IN THE PARKS

The Lord Mayor of Birmingham's War Relief Fund is again putting on a season of plays in the Birmingham Parks. This, the fifth season, opens on May 28 at Cannon Hill. After a three weeks' stay, Lightwoods and Handsworth are to be visited also for a three-week season. This year, in answer to many requests, the Erdington side of the city will be provided for by a three-week visit to Rookery Park, commencing July 30.

The plays selected are: "The First Mrs. Fraser" (St. John Ervine), "The Light of Heart" (Emlyn Williams) and "You Never Can Tell" (Bernard Shaw). A special company is being assembled and the plays will be produced by Mr. Michael Madell, of the Birmingham Repertory Theatre.

Aston Swimming Club has had the same captain ever since it was formed in 1895. At the annual meeting Mr. A. E. Brown was elected for the 50th time.

SUNDAY CINEMAS CAN BE CLOSED

1945

SUNDAY opening of cinemas for the special benefit of members of the Forces, which was authorised during the war, may be continued in places where an order was obtained, but the order may be revoked if application for a revoking order is made, under the Emergency Laws — Transitional Provisions—Bill, presented to Parliament yesterday by the Home Secretary, Mr. Chuter Ede.

JAZZ FANS

TOWN HALL

Saturday, June 14th, 1947. At 7-0 p.m.

SUPER HOT CLUB OF LONDON CONCERT

with

GEORGE WEBB'S DIXIELANDERS

HUMPHREY LYTTLETON AND HIS BAND

with Eddie Harvey, Wally Fawkes, Gerry Collins Quartet.

REG. RIGDEN TRIO TONY SHORT TRIO

Britain's Finest Jazz Men.

THREE HOURS OF JAZZ. GUEST STARS.

Watch for Opening Date of

THE HOT CLUB OF BIRMINGHAM

All Attractions organised by

LOUIS D. BRUNTON PRESENTATIONS

7, Bradnock Close, King's Heath, Birmingham, 14.

(Send your name and address and be on our Mailing List.)

BRAMPTON HAWKINS

ENTERTAINER

(Humorous Songs, Recitals, Sketches, etc.)

Open for Engagements for Concerts, Dinners, Masonic Banquets.

832 WALSALL ROAD,
GREAT BARR,
BIRMINGHAM.

THE BIRMINGHAM & DISTRICT PRISONERS OF WAR ASSOCIATION.

MISS TRIXIE O'DARE
Presents
THE SUNSHINE REVELS
in a
GRAND VICTORY SHOW
In Aid of our Funds,
at
DIGBETH INSTITUTE,
on
SATURDAY, 12th MAY, 1945.
Doors Open 6.0 p.m.
Commencing 6.30 p.m.
SEATS .. 2/-
Welcome for all Prisoners of War and Friends.

THE MIDLAND JAZZ CLUB

is now open for the Winter Season.

Meetings will be held at

WIMBUSH'S RESTAURANT,
Corporation Street, Birmingham
(Opposite Law Courts)
every Monday from 7.30 until 10 p.m.

::::

BANDS THAT APPEARED LAST YEAR INCLUDED:

THE KEN RATTENBURY QUARTET
JIM BOLTON BLIND GROUP
STAN KEELEY QUINTET
RAY FOXLEY LEVEE LOUNGERS
JOE HUDSON SEXTET

MEMBERSHIP: 2/6 per annum.

ADMISSION 1/6 :: NON-MEMBERS 2/6

Lewis's Roof Garden, c. 1948.

Midland Jazz Productions . .

SUNDAY JAZZ CONCERTS

A series of weekly **Jazz Concerts** *is to be held at the* **Aston Hippodrome, Birmingham** *throughout the autumn and winter.*

Opening date is Sunday next, 23rd October, when the bands appearing will be :

THE REVELL TERRY QUARTET
and
JIMMY HYDE AND HIS BAND

Next week, Sunday, 30th October: 1949

FREDDY RANDALL AND HIS BAND

THEATRES AND CINEMAS

19.3.47

THEATRE ROYAL
NEW STREET. B'HAM.
Matinees Daily (Tues. & Fri. excepted) 2.0 p.m. Evenings at 7.0 p.m.
TOM ARNOLD & EMILE LITTLER present
GOODY TWO HOES
FRED EMNEY
JOY HAYDEN HENRY LYTTON
JACK STANFORD SMEDDLE BROS.
CAST OF 80 ARTISTES.
Box Office Open 10 a.m. until 8.30 p.m.

ALEXANDRA THEATRE
MATS. 2 (Fri. exc.), EVNGS. 7 p.m.
SIMPLE SIMON
Mar. 31: KEEP IT DARK, a new Farce. Prior to London Production.
Apl. 7: POLISH PARADE. A Medley of Music, Ballet and Song.
Apl. 14: "WE PROUDLY PRESENT." A new Play by Ivor Novello.
Apl. 21: BALLETS JOOSS.
Apl. 28 (to be announced).
Box Office for above open 20/3/47.
May 5: Opening of Repertory Season.

REPERTORY THEATRE.
Evenings (ex. Mon.) 6.30. Matinees Wednesday, Thursday, Saturday, 2.30.
Sir Barry Jackson presents
"THE SILENT WOMAN,"
By Ben Jonson.
Box Office 10.30—7. No phone bookings.
Tuesday, April 1st: "AN IDEAL HUSBAND," by Oscar Wilde.

HIPPODROME
HURST STREET, B'HAM.
6.0. TWICE NIGHTLY. 8.15.
ARTHUR ASKEY
EDDIE GRAY
VICTOR BARNA & ALEC BROOK.
THE CYCLING D'ORMONDES.
NOR KIDDIE. JANET BROWN.
MARY PRIESTMAN.
CYNTHIA & GLADYS.
THE JAVA BROTHERS.
Box Office Open 10.0 a.m. until 9.0 p.m.

ASTON HIPPODROME
6.20 — TWICE NIGHTLY — 8.30
The Man Who Invented Shakespeare.
LEON CORTEZ
of B.B.C. "HARMONY HALL."
With SPECIAL APPEARANCE of
ARTHUR WHITE
in "VARIETY FAIR."

DUDLEY AMUSEMENTS

DUDLEY HIPPODROME
Nightly at 7.30. Mat. Sat. at 4.15 p.m.
Last Performance Saturday, Mar. 22nd.
S. H. NEWSOME presents
JACK & THE BEANSTALK.
JACK EDGE :: ROY ROYSTON.
Mon., March 24th—Nightly at 7.30.
Mats. Wed. and Thurs., 2.15 p.m.—
"THE STUDENT PRINCE."
Box Office Open 10.0 a.m. until 9.0 p.m.

COVENTRY AMUSEMENTS

HIPPODROME, COVENTRY.
(Phone 3141). This Week and Next Week. Evenings 6.45. Matinees Thursday and Saturday, 2.30.
THE ROYAL CARL ROSA OPERA,
under direction of H. B. Phillips.
Repertoire details apply Box Office.
Sun., March 23rd, 7.0 p.m.: New Midlands Philharmonic Orchestra. Conductor, Mathew Stevenson; Phyllis Sellick and Cyril Smith.
Mar. 31: Evgs. 6.45. Mats. Thurs., Sat., 2.30: 'LADY WINDERMERE'S FAN.'

WEDNESBURY AMUSEMENTS

WEDNESBURY HIPPODROME
(Phone WED. 0634).
Nightly at 7.15 p.m. Saturday 6 and 8.15 p.m.
THE MAGNET REPERTORY CO. in
MA'S BIT O' BRASS,
A Comedy by Ronald Gow.
FREE CAR PARK.

AMUSEMENTS

ICE SKATING RINK,
SUMMER HILL ROAD. CEN. 6038.
At 11.0, 2.30, and 7.30.
BOOTS AND SKATES NOW AVAILABLE FOR HIRE.

ODEON THEATRE, Warley.
SUNDAY, MARCH 23rd. NAT ALLEN WITH HIS RADIO AND TELEVISION ORCHESTRA, with NANETTE REES & JUDY DEAN.
Doors Open 6.30. Com. 7 p.m. Book Now.

ODEON
NEW-STREET.
Doors Open 10.0 a.m. Continuous until 10.30 p.m.
TEMPTATION (A)
with
MERLE OBERON,
GEORGE BRENT,
CHARLES KORVIN, PAUL LUKAS.
Screened at 11.35, 2.46, 5.57, 8.58.
Also
MR. BIG (U)
DONALD O'CONNOR,
GLORIA JEAN,
PEGGY RYAN, ROBERT PAIGE.
Screened at 10.25, 1.24, 4.35, 7.46.

GAUMONT
STEELHOUSE LANE
Continuous from 12.30 p.m.
DANNY KAYE
VIRGINIA MAYO
VERA-ELLEN
in
THE KID FROM BROOKLYN (u)
With the Gorgeous Goldwyn Girls
(In Technicolor)
At 1.50, 5.10 and 8.25.
CANDY'S CALENDAR (U)
At 12.50, 4.10, and 7.25
MARCH OF TIME No. 1 — New Series (u)

FORUM
Cont. 12.35. MID. 4549.
An A.B.C. Theatre.
SECOND BIG WEEK OF
CARY GRANT
ALEXIS SMITH
in Cole. Porter's
NIGHT AND DAY (U)
in Glorious Technicolor.
with
MONTY WOOLLEY GINNY SIMMS
MARY MARTIN JANE WYMAN
Screened at 12.55, 3.20, 5.50, 8.15.
To-morrow Continuous from 12.35 p.m.

WEST END. —— MID. 0022.
DOORS OPEN 11.45. COMM. 12.0 noon.
GRAND ALL-BRITISH PROGRAMME
JOHN MILLS,
VALERIE HOBSON,
BERNARD MILES
in
GREAT EXPECTATIONS (A)
introducing
ANTHONY WAGER, JEAN SIMMONS.
Showing at 12.0, 2.50, 5.40, 8.30.
FULL SUPPORTING PROGRAMME
At Your Service—The West End Cafe.

FUTURIST THEATRE
To-day
RAY MILLAND,
TERESA WRIGHT
in
MRS. LORING'S SECRET (A)
2.0, 5.10, 8.15
also
FREDDIE STEWART,
JUNE PREISSER
in
FREDDIE STEPS OUT (A)
12.50, 3.55, 7.0

SCALA
TO-DAY
CONSTANCE MOORE,
WILLIAM MARSHALL
in
HATS OFF TO RHYTHM (U)
12.30, 3.10, 5.50, 8.25
also
DONALD BARRY, ANN SAVAGE
in
THE LAST CROOKED MILE (A)
2.5, 4.45, 7.25

TATLER THEATRE
STATION STREET
CONTINUOUS FROM 10.15 A.M.
PRICES 10d. AND 1/8.
DUTCH VISTA

CINEMATOGRAPH EXHIBITORS' ASSOCIATION

ADELPHI, Hay Mills (A.B.C.). VIC. 1208. John Loder, Lenore Aubert, **THE WIFE OF MONTE CRISTO** (A). Also **JOE PALOOKA, CHAMP** (A).

ALBION, New Inns, HANDSWORTH.—**SEND FOR PAUL TEMPLE** (A). Anthony Hulme, Joy Shelton; **HOW DO YOU DO-O-O?** (U), Bert Gordon.

ALHAMBRA, Moseley-rd (A.B.C.). VIC. 2826. Anna Lee, James Ellison in **G.I. WAR BRIDES** (U); and Albert Dekker, **THE FRENCH KEY** (a). News

APOLLO —— TYBURN ROAD. Randolph Scott in **BAD MAN'S TERRITORY** (U). Etc. Thursday: Magic Bow (u).

ASTORIA, Aston (A.B.C.). AST. 2384. Claudette Colbert, **WITHOUT RESERVATIONS** (A); supported by Philip Reed in **BIG TOWN** (A). News.

ATLAS, STECHFORD. —— STE. 2206. **THE CHINESE BUNGALOW** (A). Kay Walsh, Paul Lukas; **THE MAN WHO LOST HIMSELF** (U). K. Francis.

BEACON —— GREAT BARR. Edward G. Robinson, **THE SEA WOLF** (A). 2.20, 5.30, 8.40; **The Shadow Returns** (a). Thurs: **Miss Susie Slagles**

BEACON, Smethwick (A.B.C.). SME. 1045. EPIC OF ARNHEM, **THEIRS IS THE GLORY** (A). Full Supporting Programme.

BEAUFORT, WASHWOOD HEATH.—David Niven, Roger Livesey, Raymond Massey, **A MATTER OF LIFE AND DEATH** (A). Sun: This is the Life (a)

BIRCHFIELD, Perry Barr. BIR. 4333. Pat O'Brien and Ruth Warwick in **Perilous Holiday** (a); **Faithful in My Fashion** (a). Thurs: Michael Strogoff.

BRISTOL, Bristol-road (A.B.C.). CAL. 1904. Robert Donat, Emlyn Williams, **THE CITADEL** (A); Kent Taylor, **Deadline for Murder** (a).

BROADWAY, Briston-street. MID. 1761. ANNA LEE, JAMES ELLISON in **G.I. WAR BRIDES** (A), and **FRENCH KEY** (A).

CAPITOL, WARD END.—Rex Harrison, Diana Churchill in **SCHOOL FOR HUSBANDS** (A); Laurel and Hardy in **FLYING DEUCES** (U).

CARLTON, SPARKBROOK. SOU. 0861. STEWART GRANGER, PHYLLIS CALVERT in **THE MAGIC BOW** (U). Full supporting programme.

CASTLE BROMWICH CINEMA. — Karen Morley, Jim Bannon, Jeff Donnell in **THE UNKNOWN** (A); also **Blondie Knows Best** (U).

CLIFTON —— GREAT BARR. **A MATTER OF LIFE AND DEATH** (A) (Tech.) 5.40, 8.20. Full Support. Sun.: Higher and Higher (U).

CORONET, SMALL HEATH. VIC. 0420. Olivia De Havilland, Lew Ayres, **THE DARK MIRROR** (A); **THE BAXTER MILLIONS** (U), Fay Holden.

CROWN, Ladywood (A.B.C.). EDG. 1122. Paul Kelly, Douglas Fowley, **GLASS ALIBI** (A); Philip Reed and Hilary Brook, **BIG TOWN** (A). News.

DANILO, LONGBRIDGE. PRI. 2470. Betty Hutton in **CROSS MY HEART** (A) at 2.15, 5.35, 9.0; Will Fyffe in **Rulers of the Sea** (U) at 3.45, 7.10.

DANILO, QUINTON. WOO. 2562.—Michael Wilding in **CARNIVAL** (A), with Sally Gray; also **CLUB HAVANA** (A).

EDGBASTON, Monument-road (A.B.C.). EDG. 3273. Van Johnson & Keenan Wynn, **NO LEAVE NO LOVE** (U); also **CHILDREN ON TRIAL** (A).

ELITE —— HANDSWORTH NOR. 0665. For Six Days. Birmingham's Own Hazel Court, Michael Wilding in **CARNIVAL** (A).

EMPIRE, SMETHWICK. SME. 0757. John Loder, Lenore Aubert in **THE WIFE OF MONTE CRISTO** (A); also Tom Neal in **CLUB HAVANA** (A).

GAIETY, COLESHILL ST. (A.B.C.). CEN. 6649. **WEEK-END IN HAVANA** (U), in Colour; **RENDEZVOUS 24** (A).

EMPRESS, Sutton (A.B.C.). Sut. 2363. Robert Donat, Emlyn Williams in **THE CITADEL** (A). And Full Supporting Programme.

ERA CINEMA, BORDESLEY GREEN. Robert Young, Helen Gilbert, Lee Bowman, and Charles Coburn in **FLORIAN** (U).

GLOBE, ASTON. —— AST. 0652. John Wayne in **DAKOTA** (A). **HANDS ACROSS THE OCEAN** (U).

GRAND, Soho-road, HANDSWORTH.—**FLIGHT FROM FOLLY** (A), Pat Kirkwood, Sydney Howard; also **ELMER'S OTHER TALE** (A).

GRAND, Alum Rock-road, SALTLEY. **THE LAST OUTPOST** (A), Cary Grant; **DOUBLE EXPOSURE** (A). Chester Morris.

GRANGE, SMALL HEATH. VIC. 0434. Rex Harrison, Diana Churchill in **SCHOOL FOR HUSBANDS** (A); Laurel and Hardy in **FLYING DEUCES** (U).

GROVE CINEMA, Dudley-road. SME. 0343. **The Dark Mirror** (a), Mon. to Fri. 3.17, 6.4, 8.51; **The Baxter Millions** (u) Sun: Woman of the Town (a).

IMPERIAL, Moseley-rd. (A.B.C.). CAL. 2283. Rex Harrison, **ANNA AND THE KING OF SIAM** (A), with Irene Dunne; also **GLAMOUR GIRL** (A).

KING'S NORTON—June Haver, **THREE LITTLE GIRLS IN BLUE** (U); Philip Reed, **BIG TOWN** (A).

KINGSTON, SMALL HEATH. VIC. 2639. George Raft and Sylvia Sidney, in **MR. ACE** (A); also William Boyd, in **LUMBERJACK** (U).

KINGSWAY —— HIG. 1352. June Haver, George Montgomery, in **THREE LITTLE GIRLS IN BLUE** (U) (Tech.). Screened at 2.25, 5.35, 8.45.

LUXOR.—Gene Tierney, Cornel Wilde, **LEAVE HER TO HEAVEN** (A) (Technicolor). FULL SUPPORT.

LYRIC, PARADE.—**SMOKEY** (U) (Technicolor), Fred MacMurray, Anne Baxter; **LUCKY CISCO KID** (U), Cesar Romero.

MAJESTIC, BEARWOOD.—Mon.—Fri. 6, Sat. 5. Barbara Stanwyck, **THE BRIDE WORE BOOTS** (A); also **BIG TOWN** (A).

MAYFAIR —— PERRY COMMON. **OLD MOTHER RILEY AT HOME** (A) and **ENCHANTED ISLE**. Thurs.: Courage of Lassie (a).

MAYPOLE, King's Heath. WAR. 2051. Betty Grable, June Haver, in **THE DOLLY SISTERS** (A) (in Technicolor).

NORTHFIELD CINEMA. PRI. 1463.—Lee Bowman, **The Walls Came Tumbling Down** (a). **Personality Kid** (u). Thurs.: Claudia and David (a).

OAK, Selly Oak (A.B.C.). SEL. 0139. Bruce Bennett, **TARZAN AND THE GREEN GODDESS** (U); supported by Laurel and Hardy in **JAILBIRDS** (U).

ODEON, BLACKHEATH. BLA. 1036. Janet Blair, **TARS AND SPARS** (U) James Craig. **DANGEROUS PARTNERS** (A).

ODEON —— KINGSTANDING. **WIFE OF MONTE CRISTO** (A). **JUST WILLIAM** (U). (Last Performance 7.30 p.m.)

ODEON, PERRY BARR. BIR. 4453.—**THE PERFECT MARRIAGE** (A) Also **MEN WITH WINGS** (U). Last Complete Performance 7 p.m.

ODEON, SHIRLEY —— SHI. 1183. Cont. 2.0 p.m. Johnny Weissmuller, Brenda Joyce, **TARZAN & THE AMAZONS** (U). **One Way To Love** (u).

ODEON, SUTTON COLDFIELD.—Michael Redgrave, **The Years Between** (a). Last Perf. 7.15. Thurs.: The Perfect Marriage (a).

ODEON —— WARLEY David Niven, **THE PERFECT MARRIAGE** (A). 2.15, 5.33, 8.51. **Men With Wings** (u). Last Perf 7.0.

OLTON CINEMA.—Tom Walls, Glynis Johns, Jeanne de Casalis, **THIS MAN IS MINE** (A). With Full Support.

OLYMPIA, LADYPOOL-RD. VIC. 0124. Ralph Richardson, Edna Best, **SOUTH RIDING** (A). Sidney Toler, **THE JADE MASK** (A).

ORIENT, Aston (A.B.C.). NOR. 1615. Walter Pidgeon, Jane Powell in **HOLIDAY IN MEXICO** (U). Colour. And Full Supporting Programme.

PALACE, Erdington (A.B.C.). ERD. 1623. Robert Donat, Emlyn Williams, **THE CITADEL** (A) And Full Supporting Programme.

PALLADIUM, Hockley (A.B.C.). NOR. 0380. Karen Morley, Jim Bannon in **THE UNKNOWN** (A). Also **THE MAN WHO DARED** (A).

PAVILION, STIRCHLEY (A.B.C.). KIN. 1241. Walter Pidgeon, Jane Powell, **HOLIDAY IN MEXICO** (U). Colour. And Full Supporting Programme.

PAVILION, Wylde Green (A.B.C.). ERD. 0224. Walter Pidgeon, Jane Powell, **HOLIDAY IN MEXICO** (U). Colour. And Full Supporting Programme.

PICCADILLY, Sparkbrook (A.B.C.). VIC. 1688. Bruce Bennett, **TARZAN AND THE GREEN GODDESS** (U); Laurel and Hardy, **FLYING DEUCES** (U).

PICTURE HOUSE, Aston Cross (A.B.C.). EAS. 0430. Sydney Greenstreet in **THE VERDICT** (A); and also **ONE EXCITING WEEK** (A).

PICTURE HOUSE, Erdington (A.B.C.). ERD. 1484. Edward G. Robinson in **THE STRANGER** (A). Also **RADIO STARS ON PARADE** (A).

PICTURE HOUSE (G.B.), HARBORNE All Week: David Niven, Kim Hunter, in **A MATTER OF LIFE & DEATH** (A) (Tech.), the Royal Command Film!

PLAZA, Stockland Green. ERD. 1048. David Niven, **MATTER OF LIFE & DEATH** (A); **CRIMSON CANARY** (A) Sunday: Behind the Rising Sun (a).

PRINCES, SMETHWICK. SME. 0221. Anna Neagle and Michael Wilding in **PICCADILLY INCIDENT** (A); also **WOMEN IN SPORT** (U).

REGAL, Handsworth (A.B.C.). NOR. 1801. Walter Pidgeon, Jane Powell, **HOLIDAY IN MEXICO** (U). Colour. And Full Supporting Programme

RIALTO, HALL GREEN. SPR. 1270. **The Adventures of Robin Hood** (u). Errol Flynn, Olivia de Havilland, Basil Rathbone. Full Support Programme (u)

RINK (G.B.), Smethwick. SME. 0950. Ingrid Bergman, **ADAM HAD FOUR SONS** (A); **DANGEROUS BUSINESS** (A). Free Car Park for Patrons.

RITZ, Bordesley Green (A.B.C.). VIC. 1070. Ida Lupino, Robert Alda in **THE MAN I LOVE** (A); Anne Gwynne, **I RING DOORBELLS** (A).

ROBIN HOOD, Hall Green (A.B.C.). SPR. 2371. Walter Pidgeon, Jane Powell, **HOLIDAY IN MEXICO** (U). (Tech.). Full supporting programme.

ROCK CINEMA, Alum Rock.—Chips Rafferty and Daphne Campbell in **THE OVERLANDERS** (U); **CLUB HAVANA** (A). Thurs.: Carnival (a).

ROYALTY, Harborne (A.B.C.). HAR. 1619. Douglas Fairbanks, **CORSICAN BROTHERS** (A); Dennis O'Keefe, **GETTING GERTIE'S GARTER** (A).

RUBERY CINEMA. Phone 193.—Bela Lugosi, Lon Chaney, in **Frankenstein Meets the Wolf Man** (H); **Easy to Look At** (U). No children under 16 admitted

SAVOY, King's Norton. KIN. 1069.—Alan Ladd, Loretta Young, **AND NOW TO-MORROW** (A); John Carradine in **FACE OF MARBLE** (A).)

SHELDON CINEMA —— SHE. 2158. Humphrey Bogart, Lauren Bacall in **THE BIG SLEEP** (A). Thurs.: CLAUDIA AND DAVID (A).

SOLIHULL —— SOL. 0398 Anthony Hulme and Joy Shelton in **SEND FOR PAUL TEMPLE** (A); **Blossoms in the Dust** (a) Greer Garson

STAR CINEMA, Erdington. EAS. 0461. **SEND FOR PAUL TEMPLE** (A), Anthony Hulme; **Come Out Fighting** (a) East Side Kids. Thurs: Devotion (u)

TIVOLI PLAYHOUSE, Coventry-road.—**THE PHANTOM** (A) with Tom Tyler, Jeanne Bates; **OUR HEARTS WERE GROWING UP** (A). Gail Russell.

TUDOR, KING'S HEATH (A.B.C.). BIG. 1161. Ida Lupino, Robert Alda, in **THE MAN I LOVE** (A); Anne Crawford in **HEADLINE** (A).

TRIANGLE, Gooch street, Birmingham **JUST BEFORE THE DAWN** (A). Warner Baxter; also **HIT THE HAY** (A). Judy Canova.

VICTORIA. EAS 0479. — Paulette Goddard, Ray Milland in **KITTY** (A); **THEY MADE ME A KILLER** (A). Thurs.: G.I. WAR BRIDES (U).

VILLA CROSS (G.B.). NOR. 0607. — The Royal Command Performance Film. David Niven in **A MATTER OF LIFE & DEATH** (A) (Tech.) 3.20, 6.0, 8.35.

WARWICK CINEMA, Acock's Green. Louis Hayward, Joan Bennett, Warren William, Alan Hale in **THE MAN IN THE IRON MASK** (A).

WEOLEY —— WEOLEY CASTLE George Raft, Joan Bennett, **The House Across The Bay** (A); **Texas Masquerade** (U). Mon. & Thurs. Cont. from 2.30.

WINDSOR, BEARWOOD. BEA 2244. Mon., Thurs., Sat. from 5. Tues., Wed., Fri. 6. Maureen O'Hara, **Spanish Main** (A); also **Scottish Symphony** (U).

WINSON GREEN. NORTHERN 1790. **Her Kind of Man** (A), Zachary Scott; **So Dark the Night** (A), Steve Geray. Thurs.: Devotion (U), Ida Lupino.

WEST BROMWICH CINEMAS

CLIFTON, STONE CROSS. STO. 2141. Boris Karloff, Lon Chaney, in **House of Frankenstein** (H). Children under 16 not admitted. **She Wrote the Book** (A)

IMPERIAL, West Bromwich. WES. 0192 David Niven, Kim Hunter, Roger Livesey, **A MATTER OF LIFE AND DEATH** (A) (Tech.), at 3.5, 5.40, 8.20

PALACE CINEMA. WES. 0358.—David Niven, Roger Livesey, **A MATTER OF LIFE & DEATH** (A) (Tech), approx. 2.40, 5.30, 8.15; **Land of the Saints** (u)

PLAZA, WEST BROMWICH. WES. 0030 Fred Astaire and Paulette Goddard in **SECOND CHORUS** (U); also Bill Boyd in **BORDERLAND** (U).

QUEEN'S. WES. 0351. Large Car Park. Paul Lukas and Jane Baxter in **THE CHINESE BUNGALOW** (A); Brian Aherne, **Man Who Lost Himself** (u).

ST. GEORGE'S CINEMA. Phone WES. 0737. Patricia Burke, David Farrar, Richard Tauber, in **THE LISBON STORY** (A).

TOWER (A.B.C.). —— WES. 1210. Cary Grant and Alexis Smith, **NIGHT AND DAY** (U). (Tech.). Life Story of Cole Porter.

Stewart Granger at the Carlton.

Danny Kaye at the Gaumont.

Jean Simmons at the West End.

HAROLD HOLT LTD. present

INTERNATIONAL CELEBRITY SUBSCRIPTION CONCERTS.

TOWN HALL.

FRIDAY, NOVEMBER 28th. at 7.0

ITURBI 21/11/47

ITURBI

ITURBI

ONLY APPEARANCE IN BIRMINGHAM OF THE GREAT PIANIST OF CONCERT, RADIO AND FILM FAME.

5/- to 15/-

ALAN PRIESTLEY, 27B, Paradise-st., BIRMINGHAM —— MIDland 0021.

TO-MORROW:

EVELYN LAYE

KENNETH HORNE

WINSTON SIMON

JAN BERENSKA AND HIS ORCHESTRA

in an ALL-STAR CONCERT in aid of the BIRMINGHAM MAIL CHRISTMAS TREE FUND, at THE TOWN HALL, BIRMINGHAM, 7 p.m.

Plans and Tickets:

8/3 7/6 6/9 5/3 4/6 & 3/- from ALAN G. PRIESTLEY, LTD., 27b, Paradise-street, Birmingham, 1.

Tickets may also be obtained at the Birmingham Post & Mail Office, New-st.

"The Happiest Days of Your Life", St Paul's Dramatic Society, St. Paul's Church, Lozells, c. 1948.

Kenneth Horne, radio personality and Birmingham businessman, appears at the Town Hall this week.

Birmingham actor as Paul Temple 21/11/47

AFTER a six-months' search, and the testing of 15 stars for a suitable candidate to play the part of Paul Temple, the famous radio detective, choice has fallen on 30-year-old Birmingham actor John Bentley.

The cast of "Mrs Dale's Diary", the popular radio serial, c. 1949.

The Springfield Cinema, Stratford Road, Sparkhill, 30th November 1949.

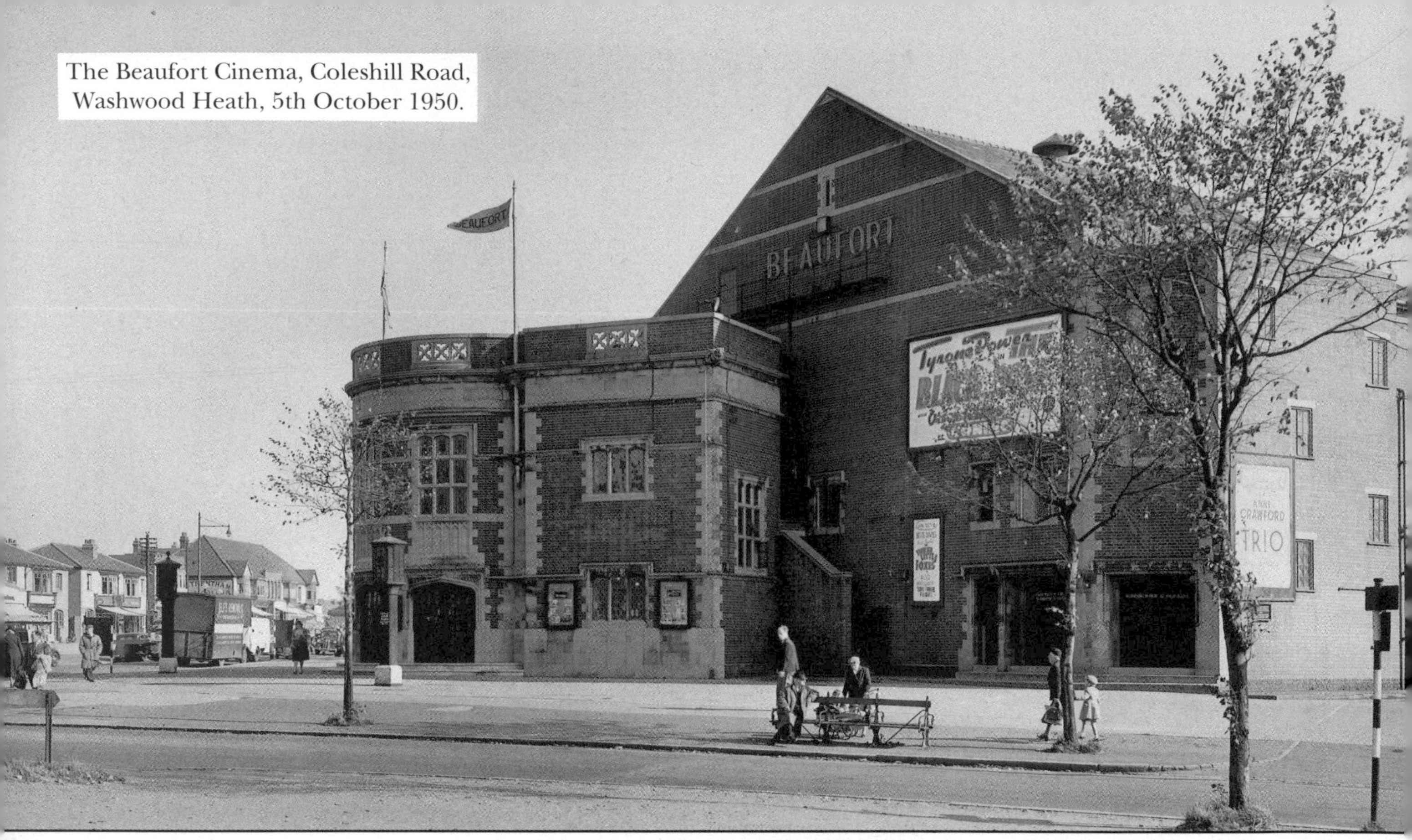

The Beaufort Cinema, Coleshill Road, Washwood Heath, 5th October 1950.

A rehearsal of "Circle of Chalk", Hall Green Little Theatre, 5th January 1951.

The Rock Cinema, Alum Rock Road, 6th February 1951.

"The Desert Song", Kingstanding Community Association Light Opera Section, 1951.

Oliver Hardy and Stan Laurel, with Lew Grade's pet goose, prior to setting out on their tour of England. As the accompanying poster in Stratford Road proclaims, they came to the City in May 1952.

THIS SELF-EXPLANATORY NOTICE appeared outside a Birmingham cinema yesterday. 2.2.52

Many Hospital Patients See TV Show

3.6.53

Visitors Allowed in for Tea

Every provision to enable patients well enough to view or to listen-in to the Coronation ceremonies was made in Birmingham hospitals. Most of them had supplemented their own television sets by borrowing others, some of which had been made available by the Red Cross and others loaned by manufacturers.

Visitors were allowed to join patients at tea and there were special menus. Usually picnic meals were served to avoid interrupting reception of the broadcasts and an evening meal with chicken or turkey provided.

St. Peter's Amateur Dramatic Society

PRESENT THEIR EIGHTH PRODUCTION

THE ISLE OF UMBRELLAS

A Comedy in Three Acts by

MABEL L. TYRRELL & PETER COKE

AT 8-0 P.M.

THURSDAY, 26th MAY 1955.

IN THE PARISH HALL ARTHUR ROAD

ADMISSION BY PROGRAMME } ADULTS 2/- CHILDREN 1/-

FREE. *BEST CATALOGUE EVER!*

of Standard, Hot, Latin-American, Old-Time ORCHS.

SERVICE - - - - by RETURN

KAY WESTWORTH'S

6 & 7 MOOR STREET, BIRMINGHAM, 4

Midland Band Leaders

NOTE—Phone: MID 6919

JACK WOODROFFE

Birmingham's largest band instrument building

119 JOHN BRIGHT STREET (City Centre)

MID 6343

Specialists in High-Quality Band Instruments.

The crowning of Kings Norton's Carnival Queen, c. 1954.

The Ritz Cinema, Bordesley Green East, 1955.

The Birchfield Cinema,
Birchfield Road, Perry Barr, 1955.

ASTON HIPPODROME
BIRMINGHAM

HIPPODROME (BIRMINGHAM) LTD
Direction........ F. J. Butterworth
Manager & Licensee........ J. Tomkinson

6.20 TWICE NIGHTLY 8.30

WEEK COMMENCING MONDAY, 5th MARCH, 1956

VARIETY

with

Bill Maynard

and

Michael Holliday

Programme ... ... Price 3d.

Forthcoming Attractions

Next Monday 12th March

LEE LAWRENCE
The Cox Twins and Variety

Monday 19th March

ISSY BONN
and Star Variety Support

Monday 26th March

SYDNEY ELGAR presents
WE NEVER CLOTHED
with Eno & Lane

Watch Out for these Attractions

"FANCY PANTS"
with JACK HAIG, MARY HARKNESS & ERIC WILLIAMS

"FOLLIES PARISENNES"
with **EDDIE REINDEER.**

Lee Lawrence.

The New Ashted Row Cinema, 11th December 1956.

The Palladium Cinema, Soho Hill, Hockley, 19th January 1956.

The Television Theatre, Aston Road North, 5th June 1956.

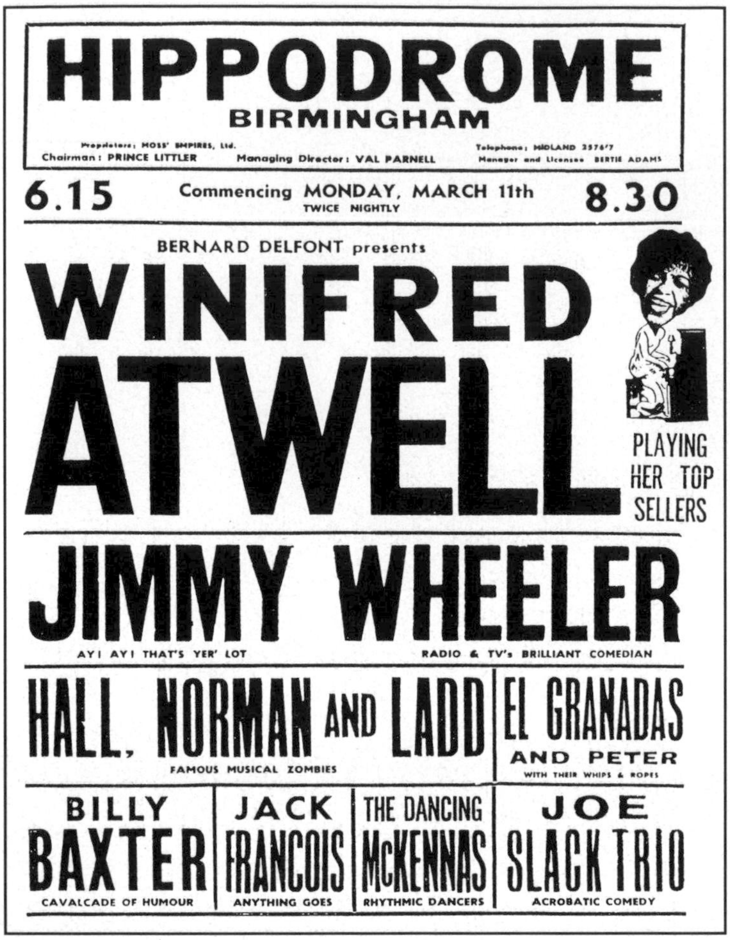
HIPPODROME
BIRMINGHAM
Proprietors: MOSS' EMPIRES, Ltd.
Telephone: MIDLAND 2576/7
Chairman: PRINCE LITTLER
Managing Director: VAL PARNELL
Manager and Licensee BERTIE ADAMS
6.15
Commencing MONDAY, MARCH 11th
TWICE NIGHTLY
8.30
BERNARD DELFONT presents
WINIFRED ATWELL
PLAYING HER TOP SELLERS
JIMMY WHEELER
AY! AY! THAT'S YER' LOT
RADIO & TV's BRILLIANT COMEDIAN
HALL, NORMAN AND LADD
FAMOUS MUSICAL ZOMBIES
EL GRANADAS AND PETER
WITH THEIR WHIPS & ROPES
BILLY BAXTER
CAVALCADE OF HUMOUR
JACK FRANCOIS
ANYTHING GOES
THE DANCING McKENNAS
RHYTHMIC DANCERS
JOE SLACK TRIO
ACROBATIC COMEDY

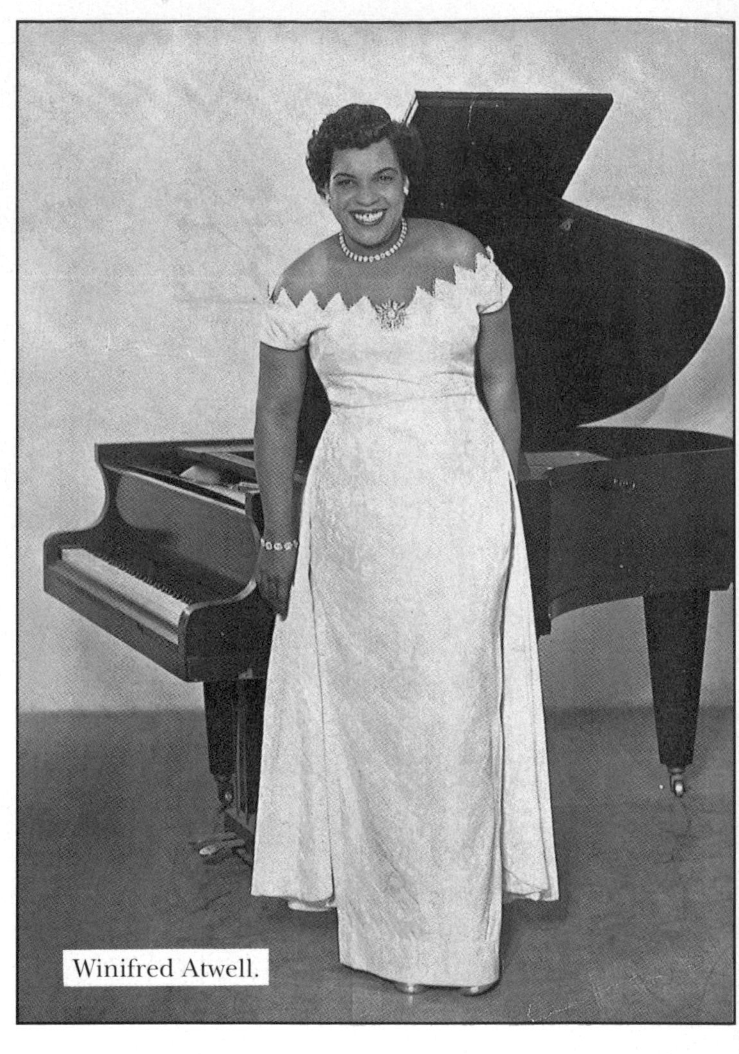

Winifred Atwell.

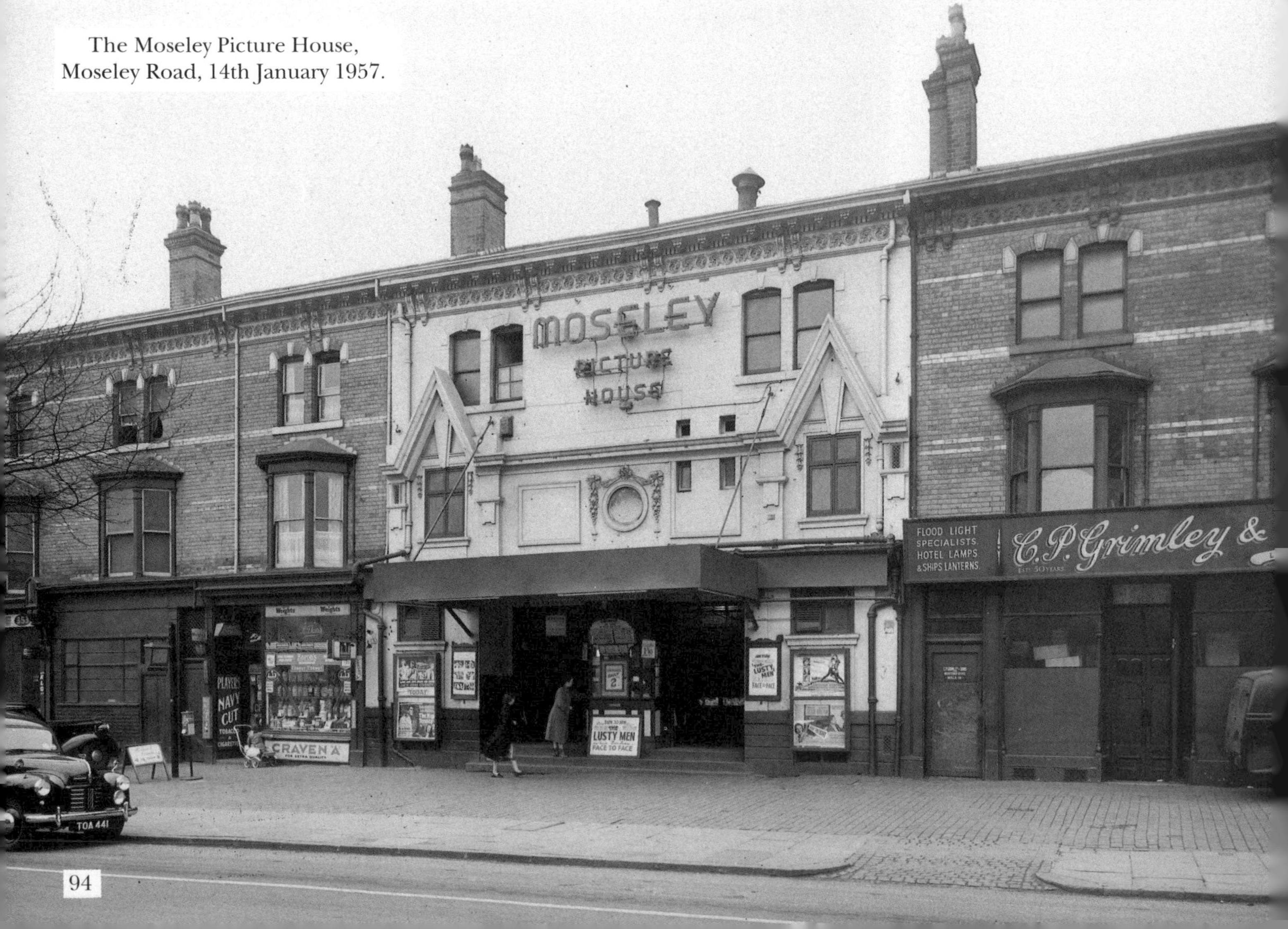
MOSELEY
PICTURE HOUSE
FLOOD LIGHT SPECIALISTS HOTEL LAMPS & SHIPS LANTERNS
C.P. Grimley &
PLAYER'S NAVY CUT
CRAVEN 'A'
LUSTY MEN
FACE TO FACE

The Moseley Picture House, Moseley Road, 14th January 1957.

Personal Service and Satisfaction 1956 Cash or Terms

Television

ALSO DOMESTIC APPLIANCES

Estimates Free

R. SATCHWELL

THE RED HOUSE

PHILLIPS STREET **Telephone: AST. 3381**

The Accordion Depot, Newton Street, Dale End, 10th April 1956.

HIPPODROME BIRMINGHAM LTD. **Aston Hippodrome** (Telephone AST 2341)

Managing Director ... ... F. J. BUTTERWORTH
Manager and Licensee ... ... J. TOMKINSON

Make your visit to the Aston Hippodrome a regular weekly one by registering at our Box Office for Permanent Seats which must be picked up not later than :— First House : 6.0 p.m. Second House : 8.10 p.m.

Telephone Bookings must also be picked up before these times.

Light Refreshments, Ices and Chocolates may be obtained from our Circle Buffet

6.20	TWICE NIGHTLY		8.30
Orchestra Stalls ...	3/6	**Dress Circle**	3/-
Royal Stalls ...	2/9	**Royal Circle**	2/3
Pit Stalls	1/9	**Back Circle**	1/9
Boxes (4 seats) ...	16/-	**Balcony** (Unreserved)...	1/6

All prices include Tax

Doctors and other patrons expecting urgent messages may leave instructions at the Box Office. Open daily from 10 a.m. to 7.0 p.m. **Old Age Pensioners at reduced rates Monday or Tuesday, 1st House**

The Regal Cinema, Soho Road, Handsworth, 14th February 1956.

The Alhambra Cinema, Moseley Road, 14th January 1957.

The Triangle Cinema, Gooch Street, Balsall Heath, 14th January 1957.

Kings Heath Theatre Club's production of "The Man With a Load of Mischief", Billesley Community Centre, October 1957.

PAT Astley was chosen out of 823 applicants for the job of new announcer for ATV in the Midlands.

Pat, aged 36, a motor engineer from Bromsgrove was chosen because they wanted "someone with a pleasant personality and no accent." 20.12.57

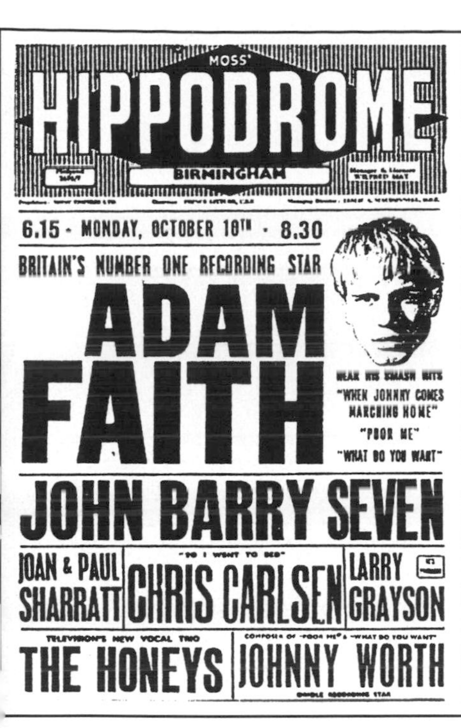

The Circle Players, Community Centre, Kingstanding, 1958.
The company celebrated 60 years of existence in 1994.

The Bournville Social Club,
Franklin Road/Maryvale Road,
Bournville, 22nd July 1958.

The Warwick Cinema, Westley Road,
Acocks Green, 24th July 1958.

ASSOCIATED TELEVISION LIMITED

cordially invite you to peep behind

"LUNCH BOX"

1,000th PERFORMANCE

where Nöele Gordon, " The Boys "
and Crew will be seen in their natural surroundings
at

THE TELEVISION THEATRE . ASTON

Doors open 12.15 p.m. *No admittance after 12.30 pm.*

Ass Tuesday, 20th September, 1960 **G** 11

Tel PLEASE NOTE, THE POLICE WILL NOT ALLOW THE PARKING OF CARS IN THE MAIN ROAD OUTSIDE THE STUDIOS.

ADMIT ONE SEATS IN CIRCLE ONLY

Bournville Dramatic Society

49th Season 1960-61

SILVER WEDDING

BY

MICHAEL CLAYTON HUTTON

High Fidelity & Photographic

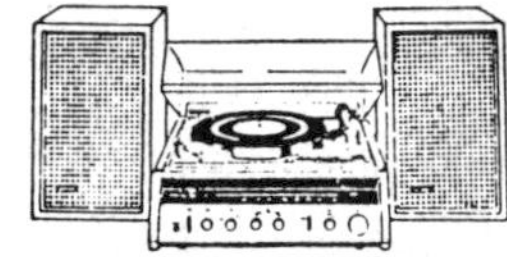

37/39 YORK ROAD
KINGS HEATH, BIRMINGHAM

Telephone 021 444 4182

SONY®

Proprietor : Colin C. Turner

The Apollo Cinema, Tyburn Road, Birches Green, Erdington, 22nd April 1959.

The British Legion Club, Hurst Lane/ Brownfield Road, Shard End, 2nd June 1959.

The BBC radio programme, "Worker's Playtime", visits the BSA, Golden Hillock Road, Small Heath, c. 1960. Philip Garston-Jones offers the show's accompanist, Harry Engleman, a sandwich, with top-of-the-bill magician, David Nixon, in centre position.

Sid James (right) seen here rehearsing with Tony Hancock for BBC television's "Hancock's Half Hour", appears in person, as well as on film, at the Forum on Tuesday, 28th March 1961.

HIPPODROME BIRMINGHAM

1961

SUNDAY NEXT, 26th March, at 5 and 7.30

THE FRANKIE VAUGHAN SHOW

BILLY TERNENT and his FULL ORCHESTRA
TONY FANE TRACY SISTERS
"HERE'S HARRY" – HARRY WORTH

Box Office 10 till 9. Telephone: MID. 2576
PRICES 10/6 — 5/-

GRAND FILM PREMIERE
MIDNIGHT MATINEE

'CARRY ON REGARDLESS' (U)

Starring
SIDNEY JAMES
CHARLES HAWTREY
KENNETH CONNOR
KENNETH WILLIAMS
JOAN SIMS
BILL OWEN
LIZ FRAZER

DAVID KOSSOF will introduce the STARS OF THE FILM
Tuesday, March 28th at 11.45 p.m. Doors Open 11.15 p.m.
TICKETS NOW AVAILABLE at LEWIS'S & CIVIC RADIO from 2 guineas to 5s.
Reduced Prices 30 or more (Reduced 2/6 each seat)
IN AID OF
THE ROYAL COMMONWEALTH SOCIETY FOR THE BLIND

FORUM CINEMA, NEW STREET

BRITISH EMPIRE CANCER CAMPAIGN
105, COLMORE ROW, BIRMINGHAM, 3. CEN. 2023

A SATURDAY SPRING FAIR
ON MARCH 25th
AT THE MEDICAL INSTITUTE
(Corner of Highfield Road and Harborne Road, near Five Ways, Edgbaston).
EVERYTHING FOR YOUR SPRING SHOPPING
11 a.m. to 5 p.m.
To be opened by
MR. LESLIE DUNN
Paul Johnson of "The Archers" and of "Midland Montage."
PROCEEDS FOR CANCER RESEARCH IN BIRMINGHAM.
Buses from City No. 3a, 12, 22 to door.
MORNING COFFEE SNACKS, AFTERNOON TEAS.

"The Quaker Girl", Lucas Theatre Group, Joseph Lucas Ltd., Great King Street, Hockley, 1961.

"Aladdin", Selly Oak Methodist Church Youth Club, Bristol Road, c. 1962.

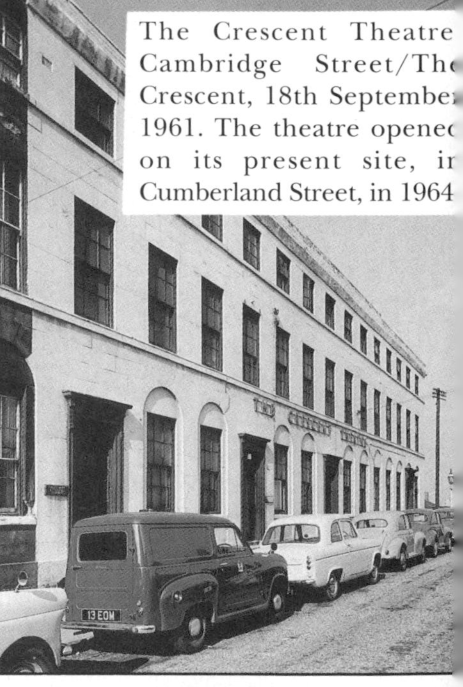

The Crescent Theatre, Cambridge Street/The Crescent, 18th September 1961. The theatre opened on its present site, in Cumberland Street, in 1964.

ROSCOMMON COUNTY ASSOCIATION

FOUR BIG NIGHTS

presenting

KILLINA CEILI BAND

appearing:

Harp Club, Walford Road .... Thursday, November 2
Selly Oak Boys' School, Oak Tree Lane .... Friday, November 3
St. Patrick's Hall, Dudley Road .... Saturday, November 4
Abbey Hall, Erdington .... Sunday, November 5

Subscription 4s.

This is the chance you have been waiting for —to hear this fabulous Irish band

1961

GOLDEN JUBILEE SEASON 1911-12 to 1961-62

THE WITCH

Translated from the Norwegian play of
H. WEIRS-JENNSEN

CONCERT HALL, BOURNVILLE

FRIDAY AND SATURDAY
FEBRUARY 23RD AND 24TH, 1962
at 7.15 p.m.

The Albion, Wheeler Street,
Newtown, 3rd June 1960.

Duke of Cambridge, Hope Street,
Highgate, 4th October 1961.

The Villa Cross Picture House, Heathfield Road, Handsworth, 28th December 1962.

The Orient Cinema, High Street, Aston, 28th June 1963.

Acocks Green group,
The Congressmen, 1963.

The Chucks beat group, from Yardley Wood,
just prior to setting out on a tour of Germany, 1964.

Sales Manager: CECIL VILES

GEORGE CLAY MUSIC CENTRE

259 Broad Street, Birmingham

Telephone: MID 0593

"THE MUSICIAN'S SERVICE FOR MUSICIANS"

The British Legion Club, Little King Street,
Hockley, 21st September 1964.

December 24th For a season until MARCH 6th.

DEREK SALBERG'S
1964/5 PANTOMIME

JACK AND THE BEANSTALK

THE PREMIER NATIONAL VOCAL TRIO

THE BACHELORS

The most daring and darling Principal Boy
JOY TURPIN

The tallest giant of all
NICHOLAS BRENT

The Skeletons in our cupboard
LES OSCARS

The celebrated colourful "card" and capable comedian
COLIN CROMPTON

The gold-medal cycling champions
THE RENELLIS

The most mysterious and magical
GEORGE CAMPO
assisted by Lina Marvell

The Magnificent Mistress of Melody
PAMELA PENFOLD

The most regal "royal" and masterful monarch
ALLEN CHRISTIE

The fabulous favourite fairy
ANN SHEPHARD

The Most Loveable
LEHMISKI LADIES

The Ever-ready
JONATHON EVERETT

and

The most splendid comical acrobatic dancing dame
JACK TRIPP

Stechford Social Working Men's Club,
Northcote Road, 8th March 1965.

The Royalty Bingo Hall, High Street, Harborne, 7th July 1964.

Advertising for the Kingsway Cinema, High Street, Kings Heath, 29th September 1964.

The refreshment bar at the Town Hall,
during a typical, hectic intermission, 18th July 1965.

Plough & Harrow,
Moseley Road, Highgate, 1966.

CHIPPERFIELD'S SEVENTH INTERNATIONAL
CHRISTMAS CIRCUS
NOW AT
BINGLEY HALL
UNTIL
JANUARY 25th

Sensational New Winter Programme with more animal acts than ever before.
THRILLS, FUN AND EXCITEMENT PRESENTED TO YOU BY BRITAIN'S LONGEST ESTABLISHED SHOWPEOPLE.
Times: Daily 3 p.m. and 7.30 p.m.
Saturday 10 a.m., 2 p.m., 5 p.m., 8 p.m.
PRICES: 5/-, 6/6, 8/6, 10/6 and 12/6.
Children Half Price.
Book now at LEWIS'S BOOKING OFFICE (1st Floor)
Birmingham. Tel.: CEN. 8251.
Or BINGLEY HALL BOX OFFICE. Tel.: CEN. 1171,
And also Booking Caravan on Hill Street, near Albany Hotel.

BIRMINGHAM TRADES UNION FESTIVAL

CO-OPERATIVE HALL, HIGH STREET, BIRMINGHAM 4 (G. J. Millington—Licensee and Manager)
MONDAY OCTOBER 22nd, TO SATURDAY OCTOBER 27th, AT 7.30 P.M. 1967

'ENTER SOLLY GOLD' by Bernard Kops
Directed by Clive Barker and William T. Kotcheff

The Queens Hotel,
Queens Road, Aston, 1966.

Don't believe everything you read on signs!
The "Cabaret" and Bingo Social Club,
Wheeler Street, Newtown, 1966.

The Earl Grey,
Pershore Road, Balsall Heath, 1968.

The Eagle Inn,
Scholefield Street, Nechells, 1966.

Aston Hippodrome sadly, by this time,
no longer a theatre but used as a Bingo Hall, Potters Lane, 1969.

The Kings Norton Cinema, The Green, 11th October 1967.

Dancers from "The Black and White Minstrel Show" pose, in Hurst Street, prior to their eleven week season at the Hippodrome, October 1969.

Singer, Joe Dolan, appears at La Dolce Vita, Smallbrook Ringway/Hurst Street, July 1970.

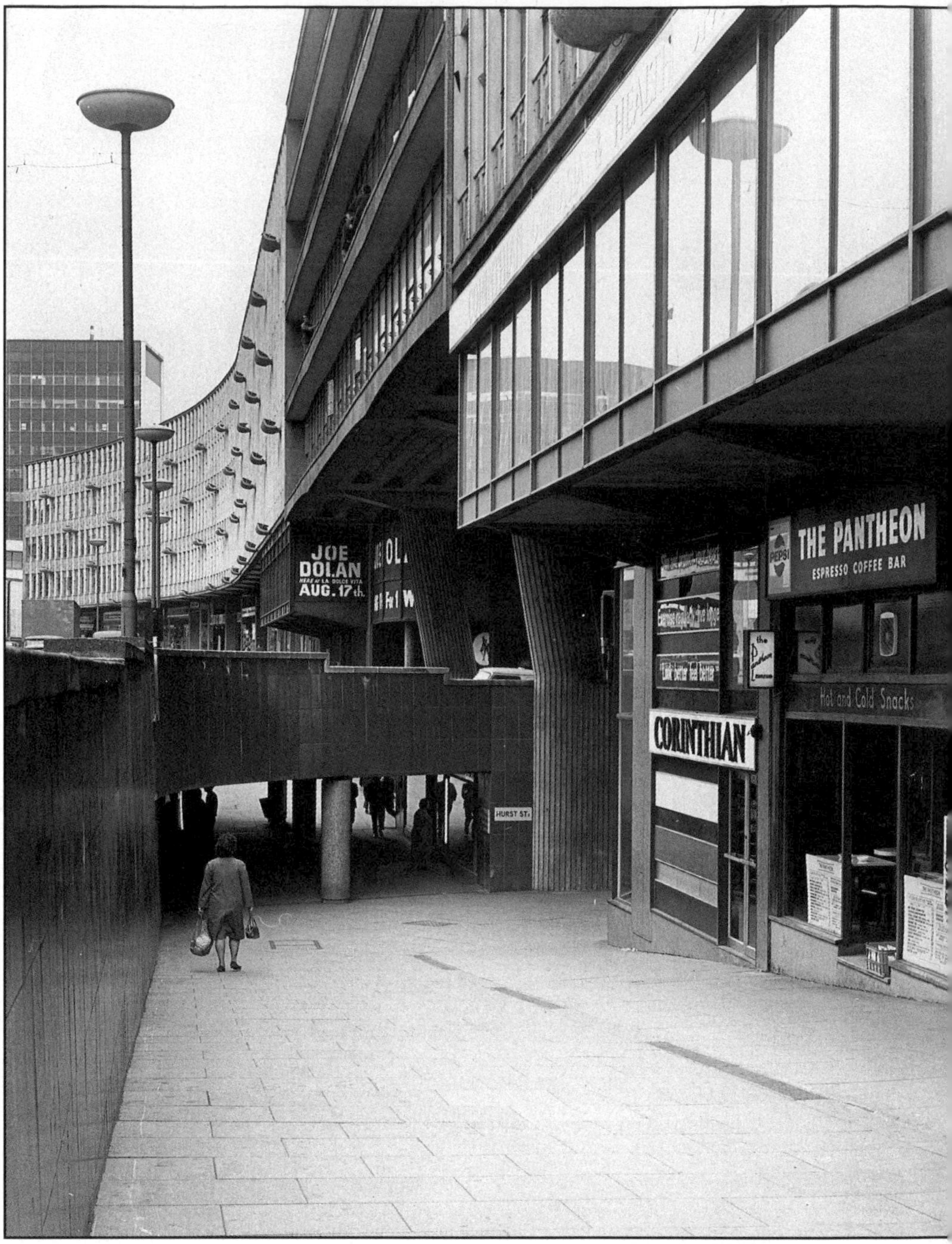

RHONDDA FACH SINGERS

1967

Holidays are over and the Welsh Societies of the Midlands look forward with anticipation to their Autumn activities. The Birmingham Cymrodorion (Welsh) Society calls its members and friends to enjoy another Male Voice Choral Concert on Saturday 14th October. The visiting Pendyrus Male Choir from the Rhondda Fach needs no introduction to the lovers of Choral music, as this is their fourth visit to the Birmingham Town Hall.

The name Pendyrus is synonymous with Arthur Duggan, their long standing conductor and after a period of marking time, under the guidance of their new dynamic conductor—Dr. Glynne Jones, they are now back in their rightful place amongst the premier choirs of Wales.

Chef & Brewer presents

THIS TENDER FLESH

a sizzling production straight from the grill

starring

The Most Delicious Steaks Ever

and featuring

Roast Chicken · Dover Sole · Fried Plaice
Roast Duckling · Grilled Gammon

with superb supporting performances by

Melon · Prawn Cocktail . Succulent Vegetables
Ice Cream · Cheese Board

in your choice of three amusing, inviting scenes:

SCENE 1
SPORTSMANS GRILL
Where quick, inexpensive meals you can really enjoy, are served from 9/- all in.

SCENE 2
FOOTLIGHTS GRILL
Ideal any time you want good food in interesting surroundings. Complete meals from 12/6.

SCENE 3
GAY 90'S GRILL
Where you'll revel in the dazzling decor of days gone by and enjoy complete meals from 14/6.

1970

Continuous performances at

THE GARDEN HOUSE

160 Hagley Road, Edgbaston, Birmingham.
Telephone Edgbaston 3449.

Playing right up till midnight, seven days a week. Matinee performances, too!
What the critics say:
"Great Value for Money . . ." "Superb Atmosphere . . ."
"Delicious Food" "Another Chef & Brewer triumph"

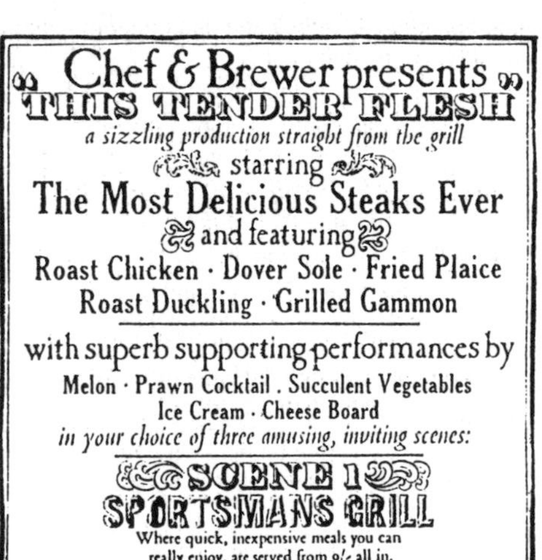

BROADSIDE FOLK! 1970

JEREMY TAYLOR

THIS SUNDAY at 8 p.m.
CROWN, STATION STREET, B'HAM.
HARVEY ANDREWS
JASPER CARROTT

JEREMY TAYLOR

1970

NEXT Saturday sees the fulfilment of a life-long dream for Birmingham-born singer David Hughes.

"He will accomplish it by being the soloist with us," says a City of Birmingham Symphony Orchestra spokesman.

"As a young man he used to earn extra pocket-money by acting as a steward at our Birmingham Town Hall concerts.

"His dream of singing with us advanced a step in 1964, when he abandoned his highly successful career in light music to become an operatic singer.

"He has sung many roles with the Welsh National Opera Company, and appeared for them, with us accompanying, at the Alexandra Theatre, Birmingham, 18 months ago.

"He will be singing extracts from one of his best-known roles, Don Jose in Bizet's 'Carmen' in our Town Hall concert on Saturday."

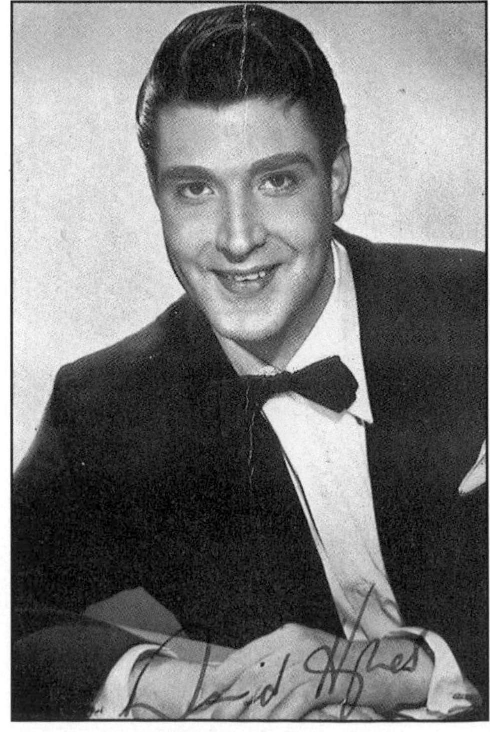

David Hughes.

Ivy Benson (left) with two members of her band.

A BIRMINGHAM society today released figures that show that their "cost of singing" has risen from £92 in 1960 to something approaching £800 in 1970.

And, although they are in the musical show business, they are not one of the Birmingham area's big money societies.

They have tried to cut costs where possible by making costumes and scenery and, more often than not, because they have been presenting Gilbert and Sullivan, they have escaped royalties.

But today's breakdown of production costs and income over ten years, drawn up by Tinkers Farm Opera Company, shows dramatically how the £ s. d. of Do-re-me is changing.

American bandleader, Harry James, brings his big band to the City, Town Hall, October 1971.

The Gaylord Club, Miles Street, Small Heath, 8th December 1971.

Christmas entertainment
provided by Cadbury's staff, c. 1972.

Paul Henry
starring in "Crossroads"
as the hapless Benny.

Tidying up time at Crossroads' motel, 1973.
Noele Gordon gives Alton lessons in sartorial elegance, shortly after he had demolished Mrs Bullock's cottage. "Crossroads" was one of the first major television soaps and a great hit for ATV.

Flamenco dancing, Los Canarios Restaurant, Albert Street, 16th January 1973.

GEORGE WILSON

BRIAN SHEPPARD

TINA WILSON

PAUL GILLINGHAM

KEITH HAYES

ROB GOLDING

SUE TODD

MIKE STEWART

MIKE HENFIELD

TONY BUTLER

TREVOR REID

JOHN RUSSELL

BRMB PERSONALITIES

PETER WINDOWS

ALAN LEIGHTON

GEORGE FERGUSON

ED DOOLAN

JOHN HOWARD

LYNDA MONK

JOHN HEDGES

NORMA SCOTT

ROBIN VALK

ALAN NIN

BRIAN SAVIN

KEVIN MORRISON

'Bunter' wins

"Billy Bunter," alias Mrs. Pat Dover, won a fancy dress parade at the Top Rank Club in Kingstanding. Mrs. Dover, of Collingwood Drive, Great Barr, who carried a huge currant bun, won £5. Second was Mrs. Anne Hewlett, of Plants Close, Sutton Coldfield, who was "crippled with V.A.T." She won £3. 1973

Sutton Coldfield bandleader, Norman Phillips, 1974. These days Norman is a highly successful entertainment agent.

Welcome to

MITCHELLS & BUTLERS

REGION 'C'

"PUB FUN"

TALENT CONTEST FINAL

on

TUESDAY, 26th MARCH, 1974

Commencing at 8.30 p.m.

at

HUNTERS MOON, COLESHILL ROAD, CASTLE BROMWICH

THE PANEL OF JUDGES

ALTON DOUGLAS	—	A.T.V. Comedian from the "Golden Shot."
GEORGE BARTRAM	—	The International Booking Agent.
"JUDGE" JEFFRIES	—	A.T.V. "Golden Shot."
JUNE JEFFRIES	—	A.T.V. "Golden Shot."
DAVE ISMAY	—	From the "Comedians", currently appearing at The "Hunters Moon."

For many citizens one of life's greatest pleasures is to read a book. Simply because it is such an architectural joy, we have chosen the Bloomsbury branch to represent all Birmingham's libraries. Nechells Parkway, January 1974.

"The White Horse Inn", The Forward Operatic Company, Birmingham Hippodrome, 1975.

The Castle Bromwich Theatre Group performing
"The Day After the Fair", Arden Hall, Water Orton Road, 1976.

SHAMROCK CLUB TUG OF WAR TEAM

DANCE & DISCO

to be held on
FRIDAY, JUNE 17th 1977.
AT THE SHAMROCK CLUB
£60 Raffle Prize Donated By The B. I. Line.
LATE BAR ADMISSION 60p

B'ham and District Variety Artistes Social Club
47, Trinity Road, Aston, Birmingham. 6.
Will be holding their Shop Window on Tues. Sept 29th. and in future the last Tuesday in
EVERY MONTH AT 8 p.m.
Entertainment Secretaries are invited. Artistes who wish to appear on future shows contact JIM HEALEY, Tel : NOR 2444 or 0382

Starring in a midnight matinee at the Alexandra Theatre, Chris Tarrant, Peter Tomlinson, Patrick Cargill, Jim Davidson and Frank Ifield, 9th February 1977. The cat is played by Terry Doogan.

The Moody Blues, 1978.

Comedian, Jimmy Marshall, Kings Nightclub, Hamstead Road, 29th April 1977.

The Record Breakers line-up

5.00-5.30 'Now They're Gold'
– says goodbye to the Hits of the last few weeks.

5.30-6.00 Pop Opinion Poll
"Air" your own views on the New Releases with Janice (Give it foive) Nichols. Tel: 021-359 4011

6.00-6.30 The BRMB Top 20
– We only play the records that are going up!

6.30-7.00 Record Breakers Competition
You predict the fastest rising record in next week's Top 20. There's fabulous prizes to be won! Entries to Box 555 Birmingham B6 4BX

BRMB
RECORD BREAKERS
So fast – it leaves
the TOP 20 behind!

24 HOUR RADIO
261 Metres Medium Wave
94·8 VHF Stereo.
Sounds Friendly!

The Celebrity Restaurant, King Alfred's Place, 5th March 1976.

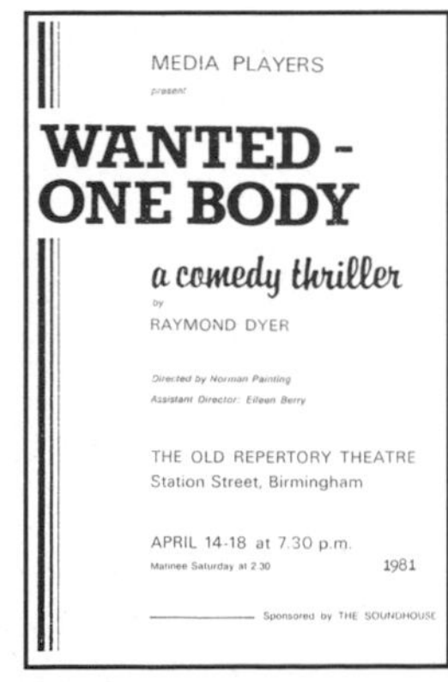

The Queen is about to meet "Pebble Mill Today" presenter, Marian Foster, BBC, 18th November 1981. To Marian's right are her fellow-presenters Bob Langley and the bearded Donny Macleod. Dame Vera Lynn can be seen on the extreme right of the picture.

A musician's eye-view of the audience as the Peacock Jazz Band play at the Botanical Gardens, 25th July 1982.

Members of Northfield Amateur Operatic Society break off from rehearsals for "Kiss Me Kate" to sing carols and raise money for The Birmingham Mail Christmas Tree Fund, Grosvenor Shopping Centre, Northfield, 17th December 1983.

Belly dancer, Leila, meets her audience, Dionysos Greek Restaurant, Broad Street, 8th December 1981. Children from all over the City were invited to a Christmas party to help celebrate the "International Year of the Disabled".

Flappers from the Phoenix Players, of Castle Bromwich, prepare to travel in a 1920's bus to entertain shoppers in Sutton Coldfield, to promote their new show "No, No Nanette", 7th August 1982.

Santa Claus climbs a golden ladder, six floors, to the top of Lewis's to announce his forthcoming presence in the toy department, 28th October 1983.

Bandleader, Freddie New and two of his band, liven up the proceedings in the Bull Ring Market, as part of the VE Day 40th anniversary celebrations, May 1985.

The Crescent Theatre Players in costume for the musical "Chicago", April 1984.

BRMB disc jockey Les Ross (right) was the toast of Mr Laurie Evans, deputy managing director of Bristol Street Motors.

They celebrated ten years of Les presenting BRMB's breakfast-time show.

Now Les has his sights set on beating Terry Wogan's record of 11 years for the longest-running radio show. 29.3.86

The Birmingham Repertory Theatre, Broad Street, April 1986.

Simon Rattle and the City of Birmingham Symphony Orchestra, 26th May 1987.

"Charlie Girl" is about to open at the Hippodrome, Hurst Street, 17th December 1987. In descending order we find Doreen Wells, Mark Wynter, Nicholas Parsons, Paul Nicholas and Bonny Langford.

All Brummies together – Malc Stent and Don Maclean give Maggie Moone the push, during rehearsals for their pantomime, Old Rep Theatre, Station Street, 13th December 1990.

The Lord Mayor of Birmingham
COUNCILLOR HAROLD BLUMENTHAL
requests the pleasure of your company

Victorian Entertainment

in the Banqueting Room of the Council House, Birmingham,
on Friday, 13th January, 1989 between 1700 hours and 1900 hours
on the occasion of the enactment of a visit to Birmingham of Queen Victoria
and at a Buffet Supper
in the Edwardian Tea Room, Museum and Art Gallery at 2130 hours

To be presented upon arrival *Carriages at 2300 hours* *Admit Two*

The 21st Anniversary Celebration

of the

Waterworks Jazz Club

on Saturday, 9th November, and Sunday, 10th November, 1991
at 20 Waterworks Road, Edgbaston, Birmingham
from 8-30 pm. to 11-30 pm.

Duran Duran, 1993.

24.11.92

BIRMINGHAM musician, entertainer and author Alton Douglas will be talking about himself, his work and his books at Sutton Arts Theatre, in South Parade, Sutton Coldfield, tomorrow evening.

He will introduce some of the music which has marked milestones in his life.

KALAMAZOO

Kalamazoo-Telethon 1992

on Saturday 18th July 1992
at Kalamazoo, Northfield

Leo the Lion's
Circus
ADVENTURE
NEW BIG TOP SPECTACULAR
IN AID OF Cardiac Unit, Queen Elizabeth Hospital
KINGS NORTON
KINGS NORTON PLAYING FIELDS, PERSHORE ROAD SOUTH
Friday 2nd October to Sunday 4th October 1992
Showtimes: Friday 5.00 & 7.30 pm;
Saturday 2.30, 5.00 & 7.30 pm;
Sunday 2.30 pm.

THIS TICKET ADMITS ONE PERSON AT HALF PRICE

CREDIT CARD BOOKINGS 0831 506459 or (0260) 271145

Midland Optical Banquet

THE TERRACE SUITE
BIRMINGHAM BOTANICAL GARDENS
EDGBASTON, BIRMINGHAM.

Tuesday 31st October 1989

The Players, United Reformed Church, Holly Lane, Erdington, during a performance of "The Railway Children", October 1993.

Ronnie Scott, whose Broad Street Jazz Club has added so much to the City's night life, 17th February 1994.

Dave and Gaynor Sandall, Chairman and Treasurer of the Tony Hancock Society, with just a part of their collection of Hancockian memorabilia, Acocks Green, June 1993.

Eric Clapton, NEC, 1993.

Nigel Kennedy, Symphony Hall, 24th March 1994.

Jasper Carrott gives the signal for his BBC series "The Detectives", 1994.

Tony Butler.
Although our photograph shows him in his Radio WM days he can now be heard on the Extra-AM station.

Jenny Wilkes.

Perminder Khatkar.

Gordon Astley, Radio WM.

Ed Doolan, Radio WM.

Prizewinners and finalists, in the Senior Star talent competition, Bull Ring Markets, 23rd December 1986.

ACKNOWLEDGEMENTS

(for providing photographs, for encouragement and numerous other favours)

David Abbotts; Neil Allen; Ron Allso; Gordon Astley; Aston Villa Football Club; John Barnsley; BBC Radio WM; Birmingham City Council, Dept. of Planning and Architecture; Birmingham City Football Club; Birmingham and Midland Museum of Transport, Wythall; Birmingham Post & Mail Ltd.; Jim Boulton; Chuck Botfield; Alan Brookhouse; L.S. Canty Silkscreen & General Printer; Dave Carpenter; Jasper Carrott; Castle Bromwich Theatre Group; Margaret Clarke; Joan Collier; David and Pauline Conway; Al and Beryl Cooke; Alan and Brenda Cronshaw; John and Jacqueline Coxell; Annette Dickers; Des and Ivy Done; Harry Engleman; Brian Ennis; Geoff and Peggy Farnall; Mike Farrell; Pat Giles; David Goodyear; Reg Gower; Peter Gupwell; Tony Hancock Society; Handsworth Historical Society; Val Hastings; Maggie Hatch; Clive Hawkins; Highfield Productions; June Hooley; John Houghton; Anne Jennings; Abel Johnson; Alan and Jean Johnson; Dave, Thelma and Tom Jones; Kynoch Rugby Football Club; Gina Manly; Harry Matts; Niels McGuinness; Pat Mills; Dennis Moore; Dick Moore; Northfield Amateur Operatic Society; John O'Keefe; One Stop Printshop; Perry Beeches Junior School; The Players (Erdington); David Potts; Dave Pucci; Eric and Dorothy Reeves; The Rockin' Berries; Dave and Gaynor Sandall; Keith Shakespeare; Keith Smart; Kath and Charles Smee; Alan Smith; Colin and Val Smith; Norman and Josie Smith; Smith's Imperial Coaches; Brian Steel; Sutton Coldfield Town Football Club; Maurice Tedd; Brian and Jan Thompson; Jill Treadwell; Roger Tufnell; Jean Vaughan; Rose Vizor; Jack and Gwen Wakeman; Joan Wanty; Warwickshire County Cricket Club; Albert and June Watkins; Christina White; Bob and Joan Wilkes; Rosemary Wilkes; Sid Willmore.

Please forgive any possible omissions. Every effort has been made to include all organisations and individuals involved in the book.

Back Cover:	Top left:	One of Birmingham's finest comedians, Winson Green's Bob Hatch, appears at Dymchurch Holiday Camp, Kent, Summer 1963.
	Top right:	Sutton Coldfield singing duo, Geoff and June ("With a song and a smile"), 1974. As well as being a most accomplished act, they also worked as score adjudicators for ATV's "The Golden Shot". Geoff was always referred to by Bob Monkhouse and Charlie Williams as "Judge Jeffries".
	Bottom:	Entertainer, Roy Castle, proclaims the re-opening of the Bull Ring Markets, 1st April 1983. The area had just undergone a £110,000 face-lift.